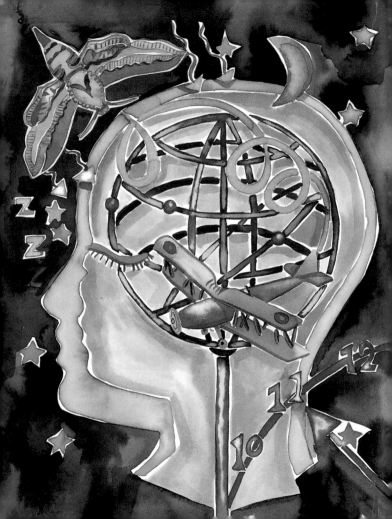

# Secrets of
# DREAMS

## CARO NESS

A Dorling Kindersley Book

Dorling  Kindersley

LONDON, NEW YORK, SYDNEY, DELHI, PARIS,
MUNICH and JOHANNESBURG

This book was conceived, designed, and produced by
THE IVY PRESS LIMITED,
The Old Candlemakers,
Lewes, East Sussex BN7 2NZ

**Art director** *Peter Bridgewater*
**Editorial director** *Sophie Collins*
**Designers** *Kevin Knight, Jane Lanaway*
**Project editor** *April McCroskie*
**Editor** *Clare Haworth-Maden*
**Picture researchers** *Vanessa Fletcher, Trudi Valter*
**Photography** *Guy Ryecart*
**Illustrations** *Sarah Young, Andrew Kulman, Michael Courtney, Michaela
Blunden, Ivan Hissey, Madeleine Hardie, Liz Cooke, Tony Simpson*
**Three-dimensional models** *Mark Jamieson*

First published in Great Britain in 2001 by
DORLING KINDERSLEY LIMITED,
9 Henrietta Street, London WC2E 8PS

A CIP catalogue record for this book is
available from the British Library

ISBN 0 7513 3557 6

Originated and printed by
Hong Kong Graphics and Printing Limited, China

see our complete
catalogue at
**www.dk.com**

# CONTENTS

*I am at the seaside, wandering along amongst the debris that a recent storm has thrown up on the beach. The sun is sinking. I start to collect small, green, pebble-like objects that I find amongst the driftwood and seaweed. I feel compelled to put one of them in my mouth.*

**Total recall**
*It is important to write down every detail of your dream that you can remember as soon as you wake.*

# HOW TO USE THIS BOOK

This book comprises six sections. The first part describes the physiological changes the body undergoes while asleep and dreaming. The second section explores theories on dreams through history to the present. The third section discusses the types of dream that you may encounter. The fourth and fifth sections encourage you to begin exploring your own dream work by recording your dreams and learning how to interpret some of the principal dream themes. The sixth, and final, section supports any intention you may have to develop and further your understanding of dreams and sleep.

### Further Information

The information presented within the pages of this book is intended to inform you about the nature of the dream state, and to explain the numerous theories related to dreams and their analysis.

It allows you to draw your own conclusions about each analyst's contribution to dream interpretation and to explore the field further. However, you should always remember that your dreams are unique to you and that you alone are truly qualified to interpret them correctly.

**The dream state**
*The first section of the book describes what happens to the body and the brain during sleep.*

**Dream analysts**
The book discusses the theories of some of the leading dream analysts, past and present.

**Dream work**
This section explores some of the techniques used recently to interpret dreams, both individually and in groups, and to help those suffering from chronic traumatic nightmares.

**Dream imagery**
The book examines some of the common dream themes and their interpretation by different analysts.

# Introduction

**Sweet dreams**

*Snug and safe in a warm bed, a small girl falls to sleep and dreams of being a princess on horseback.*

Parents often encounter the problem of their children not wanting to go to sleep. There is always a good reason: "I'm still hungry!" or "I need to read my book for school", or "It's still light!". The trouble is that most of us can remember only too well that we were the same when we were young. Sleeping seems like a monumental waste of time to a child when there is something better to do; a bicycle to ride, games to play, or a favourite television programme to watch. But the discovery of dreaming changes all that.

## Buried treasure

While your mind and body rest and recuperate, your dreams take you into numerous weird and wonderful situations. You can be the leading character in your own play.

You can soar and dive like an eagle, swim like a fish, leap buildings, defy space, time, and gravity. You can be hero, or villain, or both. You can make up for all your real or imagined inadequacies. In dreams you are not required to suspend your disbelief because in this parallel universe the impossible and absurd seem effortless, real, and totally believable.

As you grow older, you begin to understand that not only does your mind take you on these wonderful adventures, it also seeks to give you vital information that you have lost or ignored during the day. The problem is that often these messages are conveyed in a kind of pictorial code – the dream equivalent of a hieroglyph. This book sets out to explore the myriad theories on dreaming and why we dream, from the earliest times to current dream research. All the theories are intriguing in their own right, whether they seek to explain dreams as a form of education or as a means of dumping unnecessary information. Some theories will seem utterly right and plausible to you, others may not, but all of them will encourage you to explore this fascinating subject further. This book encourages you to set out to try to learn to interpret dream metaphors and symbols in order to better understand yourself. It may seem that the more you learn the less you know: you may find that you cannot quite master the empty chair technique and that Delaney's dream interview technique or Ann Faraday's looking glass world are more suited to your needs. You might find you want to read more about out-of-body experiences and the extraordinary tasks people can master while asleep. We can never attempt to fathom entirely the mystery of dreams, either scientifically or rationally, but it is, nevertheless, an exciting journey.

# WHAT'S IN A DREAM?

What are dreams, and why do we dream? Why do we sometimes have dreams and sometimes nightmares? Why do we have recurring dreams? Why do some people dream in black and white? Why can some people always remember their dreams and why do others forget them? What happens to our bodies when we dream? Do animals dream? We do know when we dream and how long each dream lasts. We also know what people tend to dream about. And yet, in spite of endless scientific conjecture and experiment, none of us can agree on what constitutes a dream or what our dreams are for.

# What Are Dreams?

**Clocking on**
*Human physiology has tuned itself
to depend upon the regular alternation
of light and darkness.*

The question of what dreams are
has plagued researchers and
writers for millenia. What each
of us experiences in our dreams is
unique, formed by our own history,
emotions, and observations. What
we do know is that dreams condense
experiences or memories into single,
or multiple, symbols which are vivid
and – to the dreamer while dreaming –
utterly believable and understandable.
It is only upon waking that we struggle
to interpret the messages that have been
given in symbols and that are integral
to our dreams.

### The circadian rhythm

Our bodies work on an internal clock
that is synchronized to the earth's orbit
around the sun and the subsequent
periods of light and darkness. This body
clock, known as the circadian rhythm,
consequently allows us to peak during
the day and slow down at night. Our
blood pressure, metabolism, digestion,
and hormone secretion take their cue
from this clock, and anything that
disturbs the circadian rhythm inevitably
disturbs our sleep.

### Healthy sleep

There is no doubt that sleep is good for
us. During sleep, we secrete growth
hormones, which are responsible not
only for growth, but also for tissue
repair and renewal. Those who suffer
from sleep deprivation tend to have
severe mood swings.

Scientific research also suggests that
we need to dream as much as we need
to sleep. In a controlled experiment,
members of a group of volunteers were
woken every time they dreamed. On

the first day, all of the volunteers found
it difficult to concentrate on their work.
They couldn't remember what they had
learned on the second day, and on
the third and fourth days became
increasingly moody and irritable. Some
complained of feeling very ill and some
began to hallucinate. As soon as they
were allowed to dream through the
night, they had many more dreams than
usual, and, over the following week,
awoke to renewed vigour. It is a similar
story with stressed or depressed people.
Clinical studies of a group of divorced
women, some of whom were depressed
and some of whom weren't, showed
that the depressed women needed
more time in rapid-eye-movement (REM)
sleep. Perhaps this extra time in REM
helps those under stress to adjust more
quickly to a new situation.

### More Information

Did you know that if you have a problem, you
*should* sleep on it? People who must tackle a
demanding situation the next morning spend
more time in REM sleep during the night.

**Sleeping phenomenon**
*In REM sleep, an electroencephalograph (EEG) will register brain signals that are similar to those transmitted during periods of concentration.*

# SLEEP TO DREAM?

The brain naturally produces two chemicals – serotonin and noradrenaline – that help to transmit nerve impulses within, and to, the brain. It is also thought that these two chemicals may be involved in controlling both body temperature and such brain functions as focused attention and learning. Significantly, the levels of both of these chemicals decrease during sleep, particularly during REM sleep. This means that the body is less able to transmit any external signals to the brain, and since the brain does not have to produce these chemicals in quantity, it is given the opportunity to rest and refresh itself.

## The Stages of Sleep

There are four levels of sleep which recur in 60–90 minute cycles throughout the course of the night. When REM sleep is experienced, the sleep pattern has gone another full cycle.

 **Stage 1** Sleep is characterized by slow rolling eye movements and lasts for 1–10 minutes.

 **Stage 2** Sleep consists of low-voltage EEG waves at less than 2Hz, broken by bursts of 0.5–2-second EEG activity.

 **Stage 3** Stage 3 consists of slow EEG waves that increase until they take up 20–50% of the sleep cycle.

 **Stage 4** In this stage of the sleep cycle slow EEG waves predominate. Gradually we move back towards REM sleep.

 **REM sleep** REM sleep sees increased brain temperature and oxygen supply, fluctuation of heart rate, and irregular breathing.

In REM sleep rapid movement is apparent behind the closed eyelids

The heart rate fluctuates and breathing is irregular

Body movement is rarely made in REM sleep

### Dream debate

There is an intriguing debate regarding the contribution of serotonin – in particular, to sleep. Serotonin is thought to suppress hallucinatory episodes, so it is argued that the body's deliberate reduction of it during sleep increases our chances of dreaming. You could therefore conclude that you sleep only so that you can dream.

# The Rhythms of Sleep

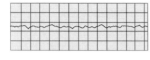

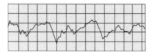

**Brain waves**

*The upper diagram shows a brain wave while awake, the lower diagram the brain wave of the same person in REM.*

Whether you are a heavy sleeper, a light sleeper, or even an insomniac, research has shown that, once you have gone to sleep, your slumber will follow a set pattern every night.

Each person experiences four different levels of sleep, measured by scientists in terms of brain waves and general physiological activity. During the first ten minutes or so, you will hover in a twilight zone, neither conscious nor unconscious. Gradually, within the first hour, you will drift deeper and deeper as you descend through each stage of

sleep until you reach level four. At this level, you are at your most relaxed and in the deepest sleep of the night. Your heartbeat and breathing are slow and regular, your blood pressure and body temperature have decreased, movement is almost non-existent, and the electrical activity in your brain has been reduced. At least 45 minutes into sleep, you reverse your journey and begin to move back up through each level until you reach level one again. As you do this, your body tends to change position, your pulse accelerates and your breathing and blood pressure quicken. You seem very close to stirring, your brain waves are close to their waking state, and yet you are now often harder to wake than you would be during level-four sleep.

## Paradoxical sleep

This re-entry into level-one sleep is sometimes referred to as "paradoxical sleep", because it defies logic to some degree. It is more commonly called "rapid-eye-movement", or REM, sleep because during this stage your eyes can be seen moving rapidly up and down, and from side to side, behind your closed eyelids, as if you were following the action. It is during REM sleep that we dream, although NREM (non-rapid-eye-movement) dreams are known to occur. The first REM episode usually lasts only 5–10 minutes, but a high proportion of people aroused during this time report particularly vivid dreams.

NREM and REM sleep will subsequently alternate in a cycle that takes an hour to 90 minutes to complete, and that repeats itself four to seven times throughout the night. As you sleep, each of your deep-sleep states becomes shallower and your REM states progressively longer, culminating in the longest period of REM, which occurs just before you wake.

### More Information

On average we spend 20–25 years of our lives sleeping, and 5–7 of those are spent dreaming in REM sleep.

# THE BRAIN AND DREAMING

Your brain is divided into two hemispheres that are connected at the centre by a bundle of nerve fibres. The left side of your brain, which governs analytical and rational thought and communication, controls the right side of your body. The right side of your brain controls the left side of your body and deals with intuitive and imaginative thought.

**Magic**
*The right hemisphere of the brain is more imaginative and is used to analyse patterns and for skills such as recognizing faces.*

**Logic**
*The left hemisphere is very good at logical thought and is used particularly for linguistic skills.*

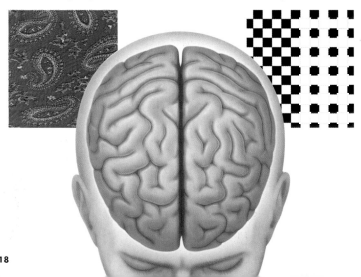

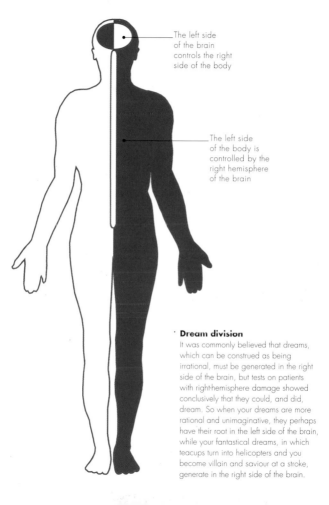

The left side of the brain controls the right side of the body

The left side of the body is controlled by the right hemisphere of the brain

### Dream division

It was commonly believed that dreams, which can be construed as being irrational, must be generated in the right side of the brain, but tests on patients with right-hemisphere damage showed conclusively that they could, and did, dream. So when your dreams are more rational and unimaginative, they perhaps have their root in the left side of the brain, while your fantastical dreams, in which teacups turn into helicopters and you become villain and saviour at a stroke, generate in the right side of the brain.

# The Theta Rhythm

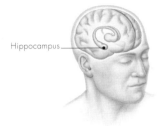

**Memory bank**
*The hippocampus lies in the temporal lobe on each brain side and is part of a system of emotion/memory sorting.*

When you dream in REM sleep, you are essentially paralysed, so that you do not make the movements you are dreaming about. Yet scientists have discovered that the theta rhythm, a brain wave pattern normally associated with survival instincts, is present in the dream state.

## The hippocampus

An American researcher, Jonathon Winson, has concluded that the theta rhythm originates in the hippocampus, where the brain processes and stores memories. He proposes that it is part of a system that gathers information that is essential for survival and rearranges it into memory during REM sleep. Winson concludes that dreams are a means of rehearsing survival strategies while the mind is free from distractions. Since the hippocampus is directly involved in short-term memory and in logging it into longer-term storage, he believes that dreaming is a means of doing just that.

## Neuronal gating

Winson furthermore proposes that by means of a process that he calls "neuronal gating", chemically active neurotransmitters can either enter, or be barred from, specific areas of the brain – the hippocampus (the memory processor) being one of them. During sleep, all of the "gates" begin to open, allowing these transmitters to enter the hippocampus. By the time that REM sleep occurs the gates are wide open, the theta rhythms are evident, and the process of memory-sorting can begin.

According to Winson's theory, you would have to "dream" your memory for at least three years before it could be moved from your short-term memory to your neocortex, the part of the brain that contains long-term memory. But if this is the case, as Winson himself says, your brain would be so enormous that you would need a wheelbarrow to carry it around.

What makes Winson's theory so interesting, however, is that studies have shown that a 24-week-old foetus is in REM sleep all of the time, while new-born babies spend 60–70 per cent of their sleeping time in REM sleep. This suggests that REM sleep is needed to allow the infant's brain to develop as quickly as possible so that it can adapt to what is, after all, a new and strange environment for it.

### More Information

French scientist Michel Jouvet found a means of "turning off" REM paralysis in a cat, so that it "chased", "killed", and "ate" the bird that it was dreaming about.

# MEMORY SORTING

In order to find an answer to the question of why we do not have vastly oversized brains in which to store our memories, Jonathon Winson proposes a system that he calls "phyletic memory". He claims that dreams process our new memories in the light of our long-term memories, rejecting those pieces of information that are unnecessary and logging those that are important. Phyletic memory in modern humans can be likened to Jung's theories on the collective unconscious. Dreams allow new memories to be evaluated against a store of core information already locked in the long-term memory, some of it dating back to primitive times. Human consciousness has evolved even further to allow us to assess the present in the light of past experience, when we are both awake and asleep.

**Prehistoric man**
*The accepted view of sleep is that slow wave sleep (SWS) developed first and REM sleep evolved later in warm-blooded animals.*

### Big brain

To support his theory, Winson cites the case of the echidna, or spiny anteater, which has a large brain out of all proportion to its size and does not experience REM sleep. His conclusion is that because it does not dream, this creature needs a bigger brain in which to store all of the survival information that it needs during its lifetime.

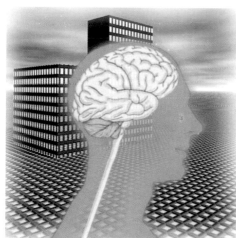

### Modern man

*REM sleep, according to Winson's echidna theory (see above), was a device that allowed modern man's large brain to continue evolving after it became limited by the size of the human head.*

# Creative and Prophetic Dreams

**Operatic inspiration**

*In 1856, Wagner confided to his friend, Liszt, that he had begun work on Tristan und Isolde, an opera that would represent his unfulfilled dreams of love.*

Dreams have often proved to be goldmines of creative inspiration. We all dream, and have the ability when dreaming to weave a magical narrative, but when we wake we lose the thread very quickly. It seems that it takes a certain kind of genius to make the spark become a flame, for there are any number of scientists, authors, musicians, and poets who have found that dreams are a fertile source of future masterpieces.

## Literary dreams

The writer Mary Shelley claimed that her novel *Frankenstein* was based on one of her dreams, and Robert Louis Stevenson maintained that the Jekyll and Hyde character was inspired by a dream about leading a double life. Samuel Taylor Coleridge dreamed the poem *Kubla Khan* in its entirety and began to write it down immediately after waking. Unfortunately, he was disturbed while doing so by the arrival of a visitor and the vision evaporated along with the rest of the poem.

Graham Greene is recorded as saying that he used to mull over the plot of his latest book just before going to bed and would find that new insights into his characters and into the plot would come to him while he dreamed. William Wordsworth consistently cited dreams as his creative inspiration, believing that during his dreams he received visits from the spirit world that gave him guidance. The novelists and

horror writers Stephen King and
Clive Barker both use their dreams as
inspiration for the plots and settings for
their popular books.

## Prophetic dreams

There are numerous prophetic dreams
on record. What would have
happened if Julius Caesar had heeded
his wife Calpurnia's dream of his
assassination several days before his
death? Similarly, a few days before his
assassination, the US president
Abraham Lincoln dreamed that he saw
his own coffin in the White House. And
during World War I the future dictator
Adolf Hitler leaped out of a trench only
minutes before it was bombed because
of a prophetic dream he had had.

### More Information

Sir Paul McCartney, former member of the
Beatles, once revealed that he had dreamed
the tune to the song *Yesterday*, one of his most
famous compositions.

**Material magic**
*The invention of the mechanical sewing machine was a technological breakthrough in mass clothing manufacture.*

# INDUSTRIAL CREATIVITY

One of the most famous recorded dreams is that of Elias Howe, inventor of the sewing machine. Howe dreamed that he was captured by cannibals and put in a huge pot full of water in which they intended to boil him alive. Realizing that the water had loosened his bonds, he attempted to haul himself out of the pot. Each time he tried, however, the cannibals pushed him back in with their spears, which had curious holes in their tips. On waking from his nightmare, Howe remembered the curious spears and eventually realized that his dream had given him the answer to the problems of speed, efficiency, and accuracy in his sewing machine: he had to make a hole in the head of the needle, through which the thread could pass.

*In his dream, Elias Howe tried to escape from being boiled alive.*

## Shadowland

The Jungian analyst Jeremy
Taylor suggests that Howe's
dream offers a perfect example
of the shadow archetype and its
creative and gift-giving ability.
The cannibals who offered the
gift of insight to Howe
symbolized the shadow.
Although the shadow is deep,
dark, dangerous, and
frightening to the conscious
mind, the unconscious mind
also contains all that we wish
for most sincerely. So, if you
strip away the frightening mask,
what you most fervently long
for will be revealed.

### Tailor-made

*Elias Howe
(1819–1867),
patented the lockstitch
sewing machine in
1846. At 250
stitches per minute,
the machine was
five times faster
than experienced
hand sewers.*

The spears with holes in their tips resolved Howe's problem.

# Levels of Meaning

**Word play**
*Dreams are full of puns and puzzles: could a basket of eggs suggest you're putting all your ideas in one basket?*

Your unconscious mind is both ingenious and playful. It uses a variety of dream metaphors, symbols, wordplay, puns, and riddles to tease, baffle, and intrigue your conscious mind. Although your dreams may appear unfathomable at first, with a little practice you will soon begin to interpret your dream messages successfully. Once you have mastered the vocabulary of dream language, the most complex of the conundrums that are posed in your dream world will seem simple to translate.

**What you see is what you get**

You may have a dream about something associated with a situation or event that happened to you the day before. For example, yesterday you were left feeling very vulnerable and alone at work because you had put all of your faith in one particular project and it had failed. The next night you dream that you are sitting all alone in the dark outside a house where a lot of people are being entertained. You are cold and hungry. All you have is a basket of eggs, but no means of cooking them.

On the surface, your dream suggests isolation and solitude, but if you look deeper, it contains hidden puns and metaphors. You are "out in the cold" because your project has been quashed. Could this be because you put all of your eggs in one basket? Did you put all of your faith in one project? Dreaming that others are eating and you are not suggests that you are feeling a lack of spiritual, emotional, and intellectual nurturing. Is this because you wilfully separate yourself from others? And what about the darkness? Are you literally "in the dark"?

As you can see, the unconscious mind plays endless tricks and games in order to force a message through to your waking self.

### A different guise

Another trick that dreams play on you is repeating the same message night after night, but in different guises. This is because your unconscious mind selects a symbol to represent the problem that is preoccupying you. If you do not understand the message the first time, the next dream will find a way of incorporating the symbol (or a related one), and will put the same information across within a different narrative.

#### More Information

David Fontana cites three levels of dreams: the non-symbolic, the mundane symbolic, and the higher symbolic, the latter corresponding to Carl Gustav Jung's "great dream" of expanded awareness and sensitivity (see pages 52–53).

# DREAMING THROUGH HISTORY

Throughout history people have struggled to interpret their dreams. The Greek philosopher Aristotle believed that dreams were augurs of illness, while the Egyptians, Romans, and Hebrews believed that dreams were messages from the gods, and the Chinese that they were messages from another world. Japanese emperors looked for political guidance in their dreams, and a special dream-incubation bed of polished stone was built in the royal palace at Kyushu. ∾ The nineteenth century brought radical new interpretations from the psychoanalysts Sigmund Freud and Carl Jung. Other influential dream analysts included Fritz Perls, Medard Boss, and Alfred Adler, who introduced the ideas of Gestalt, existentialism, and the inferiority complex.

# Eastern and Western Interpretations

**God of dreams**
*Bes, the ancient Egyptian god of dreams, was worshipped in the dream temples.*

Since the earliest times, people have been fascinated by dreams, and have left written evidence of their research and conclusions on dreams and dream meanings. The Assyrian king Assurbanipal (c.668–626BC) had a library containing a number of books on dream interpretation and a personal dream tablet, which the Greek Artemidorus later used as the chief source for his seminal work on dream interpretation, *Oneirocritica*. According to the Assyrians, dreams were the work of evil spirits that contacted the sleeper at night. These spirits could be dead people that the dreamer had known, or any evil spirit from the underworld. They were at the root of every dream, good or bad.

## The Double House

The Egyptians also took dream interpretation very seriously. Specific temples, called *serapea*, were dedicated to the Egyptian god of dreams, and the priests within devoted themselves to dream interpretation. These priests, the scribes of the Double House, were the first people to find a way of inducing dreams. Prospective dreamers would be given a herbal potion to help them sleep, and on waking the following morning would recount their dreams to the priests, who would interpret their meaning.

For the Egyptians, dreams were designed to instruct and advise, to predict the future and warn of danger, or to answer questions. Interestingly, they also put forward the theory that dreams should be interpreted in terms of opposites, so that if you dream of death you are actually dreaming of life.

## Vedic dreamers

There is evidence in the *Veda*, the sacred books of Indian wisdom, written c.1500–1000BC, that Indian philosophers recognized the different stages of sleep several millennia before William Dement, Eugene Aserinsky, and Nathaniel Kleitman discovered REM sleep during the 1950s.

### More Information

The Jews based their system of dream divination on the Egyptian model, but also took into account the history, character, financial, social, and economic situation of the dreamer.

**Dream of Maya**
A dream of the birth
of Buddha and
the ascension
into enlightenment.

# CONSCIOUSNESS
Unlike the Egyptians, the Chinese saw dreams as messages from another world, which the sleeper could interpret and use to his own advantage in this one. The Chinese believed that the spiritual soul, *Hun*, could temporarily leave the body in a dream and converse with spirits, gods, or the souls of the dead in order to educate the dreamer. Like the Egyptians and the Greeks, the Chinese and the Indians practised the incubation of dreams (see page 218). However, the Indians were concerned with the different levels of consciousness visible in dream time. They claimed that there were two states, one in this world – the world of experience – and one in the world beyond – the world of knowledge. They believed that the dream world was more real than waking life since it occupied a place in between that could touch and perceive both worlds but was not part of either.

**Dream warrior**
The sleeping Krishna
dreams of incarnating
as Vishnu, the god of
war and destruction.

**Wise illumination**

*Dreams are not only fantastical "home movies", they also
foster wisdom and enlightenment. This painting (c.1590)
portrays a sleeping giant from a Persian epic.*

# Greek Dream Interpreters

**Dream medicine**

*Hippocrates is attributed with the authorship of the first book to discuss dreams from a medical standpoint.*

The Greeks borrowed liberally from the Egyptian, Assyrian, and Jewish dream analysts. However, the Greeks interpreted dream symbolism quite differently from the Egyptians although they did, like them, believe that dreams were divine messages and they also practised incubation. Visitors to the temples would be given herbal potions to induce sleep and then encouraged to review their dreams as prophecies, but with particular emphasis on the prognosis of their physical and spiritual afflictions.

## The Greeks

All of the great Greek philosophers, among them Hippocrates, Plato, and Aristotle, were fascinated by dreams. Hippocrates (460–377BC) thought that there was a therapeutic function in dreaming, for he felt certain that dreams were "prodromal" – signals that forewarned the dreamer of impending illness or disease.

He argued that when the brain was divorced from external stimuli it became more sensitive to messages of discomfort or pain from elsewhere in the body. A dream was a way of signalling this uneasiness to the sleeper. Proof that Hippocrates' theory was close to the mark has been chronicled by countless dream analysts since.

Plato (426–348BC), in contrast, foreshadowed Freud and Jung in his belief that dreams revealed people's true natures and were the products of the innermost consciousness, symbolizing the forbidden desires that we stifle in waking life. He rejected the idea that dreams were divinely inspired, as Hippocrates believed, but, like his compatriot, he believed that they were influenced by astrological forces.

Plato's pupil Aristotle (384–322BC), who wrote three books on dream interpretation, was the first to suggest that dreams were purely the product of a physiological function. Like Hippocrates, he conjectured that dreams could be early signals of impending illness or might merely be trying to tell dreamers that their bodies were suffering some kind of discomfort (feeling too cold or too hot, for example). He believed that the immediate cause of sleep was the food that we eat. He argued that after a meal, the food that we have eaten gives off fumes that gradually enter the head, causing drowsiness and then sleep.

### More Information

Asclepius, the Greek god of medicine, was the ruling deity of more than 300 temples of dream incubation that were established in Greece from the first millennium BC onwards.

# ARTEMIDORUS

During the second century AD, the Greek Sophist Artemidorus, perhaps the most influential dream analyst of the classical world, travelled throughout the Graeco–Roman Empire collating a huge collection of writings and dream examples. He published his findings in *Oneirocritica*, a five-volume work on dreams.

**Dream deities**
*God-given dreams
were intended to
instruct and inform the
dreamer's daily life.*

## A Modern Man

In many ways, Artemidorus's approach to dreams was very modern. He was one of the first to insist that dreams had to be understood and interpreted in the context of an individual's character and profession, as well as the circumstances in which the dream took place. Although he believed that dreams were gifts from the gods, he wrote that they were intended to instruct and inform. He made an in-depth study of recurring dreams and introduced the idea that association played a key role in any dream. He also warned of the danger of too glib or literal a translation of dreams, emphasizing that the danger of this was that dreams had a habit of playing clever tricks through puns, wordplay, image associations, and metaphors. Thousands of years before Jung reached the same conclusion, Artemidorus also identified the "great dream", a dream of seminal significance which was difficult to interpret, but which the dreamer would remember over an entire lifetime.

# A Spiritual Approach

**The pendulum**

*Ayurvedic doctors believe that the mind swings between three states: lethargy, intelligence, and violent activity.*

It is fascinating to note the diversity of spiritual associations that different cultural traditions have given to dreams. In Ayurveda, the ancient Indian medicine, or "way of life", practitioners believe that every individual is made up of different combinations of the elements earth, fire, water, air, and ether. You are endowed with these elements at the moment of your conception and are governed by the elements that you inherit in equal measure from your mother and father. According to the mix of elements, your nature, or *prakrti*, is one of three *doshas*, or body types: *kapha*, *pitta*, or *vata*. In addition, your mind swings like a pendulum between three states, or *gunas: tamas* (associated with inertia, lethargy, and sleep), *sattva* (knowledge, intelligence, and purity), and *rajas* (activity, compulsion, arrogance, or anger). In order to stay well, you need to maintain a healthy balance of each of the three states.

Ayurvedic doctors observe that *kapha* individuals, in whom the water and earth elements predominate, tend to dream of water – rivers, lakes, streams, and waterfalls – and birds and flowers associated with water, such as swans or lotuses. *Pitta* individuals, whose dominant element is fire, dream of fire, thunder, lightning, and light, and see everything in bright colour during their reveries. *Vata* individuals, in whom the elements of air and space predominate, dream of flying and of mountains, hills, and desolate, dry places or plants, such as deserts or cactuses.

When you have a dream that is disturbing, an Ayurvedic doctor would suggest that the dream is prodromal and would diagnose an imbalance of *rajas*. If your dream is sexual, it is put down to an imbalance in the mind, and if your dreams are of murder, killing, suicide, or death, they are attributed to a manifestation of physical illness.

## Mohammed on dreams

Islamic dream interpretation is varied. The writer al Mas'adi believed that dreams were primarily the working of the soul. Mohammed himself maintained that dreams represented conversations between God and humans. The Islamic approach was not dissimilar to the Christian tradition, in that only the mullahs were deemed wise or worthy enough to interpret dreams.

### More Information

In the Islamic tradition, a notable man did not have to dream, since his wife, child, or slave would dream on his behalf, any message being intended for the master.

**Sinful dreams**
*The Protestant reformer Martin Luther, who was plagued by misleading dreams, later amended the satanic interpretation of dreams to suggest, more positively, that dreams could teach us by bringing us face to face with our sins.*

# THE CHRISTIAN APPROACH

In the early Christian tradition, dream analysts (who were always priests) initially took the view that dreams were sent by God to inform and command his obedient subjects. The Bible itself, as well as the writings of St. Augustine and St. John Chrysostom, are liberally sprinkled with such examples. However, St. Jerome (c. 342–420), who was tormented by disturbing dreams and their possible meanings, overturned this theory by claiming that dreams were the work of the devil. The Church adopted his theory and condemned most dreams as being satanic trickery that should be disregarded. During the Reformation, the Christian suspicion of dreaming reached new heights.

**St. Jerome's dream**
*During a near-fatal illness, Jerome dreamed that he was dragged before the Lord's tribunal, accused of being a follower of the first-century BC Roman philosopher Cicero rather than a Christian, and was severely lashed. He vowed never again to read pagan literature.*

### The Maid of Orléans

*Joan of Arc, perhaps the most famous Christian
dreamer of all, was burned at the stake for heresy
because she would not renounce her belief that her
visions came from God rather than the devil.*

# Sigmund Freud

**Prodromal dreams**
*Like Hippocrates, Freud believed dreams were prodromal, but revealed our mental not our physical health.*

In 1900 the Austrian psychoanalyst Sigmund Freud (1856–1939) published his seminal work on dreams, *The Interpretation of Dreams*, which established dreams and their interpretation as a legitimate and important part of psychoanalysis. Indeed, despite criticism of his methodology and theories, particularly his insistence on the mainly sexual nature of dreams and dream symbolism, it is fair to say that Freud's book fundamentally changed our appreciation of the mind and how it works.

## The brain machine

Freud drew a parallel between the brain and a machine, maintaining that the brain's complex neural network builds up electrical energy like a machine, and that in order to function properly it needs to discharge this electrical energy by dreaming. Freud believed that our fundamental motivation in life is fuelled by our instinctive drives, such as the survival and sexual instincts, which, although they operate on an unconscious level, control our emotional responses. He held that although there was nothing inherently wrong with these urges, there could be if the emotions linked to these instincts were frustrated or punished, predominantly in childhood, and were then suppressed. He argued that any emotion repressed in this way does not simply dissipate but lies dormant, waiting for an opportunity to escape when the conscious mind is not controlling a person's actions – that is, when the person is dreaming. As we sleep, any emotions or urges that we have suppressed during our waking moments play themselves out in dreams. However, the conscious mind still monitors the situation using what Freud called the "censor", the part of the mind that disguises the dream's true meaning by transforming images or using image association. Without the censor, Freud argued, our wish-fulfilment dreams would become so bizarre, extreme, and disturbing that we would be impelled to wake up.

## Id, ego, and superego

Freud divided the personality into the id, ego, and superego. The id represents our animal urge to act upon our instincts and desires rather than from social or cultural conditioning. The ego is our conscious mind, which mediates between the id and the superego and makes rational decisions. The superego is our conscience. Freud argued that if either the id or the superego predominated, psychological problems would occur because our feelings would remain unexpressed.

**Forbidden fruit**
*To the Christians the apple represented lust and sex, the forbidden fruit of knowledge offered by Eve to Adam.*

# FREUD ON SYMBOLISM

Freud believed that the symbolic nature of dreams is part of a universal symbolic language. He held that psychologists can learn this language and use it to interpret their clients' dreams and thus the psychological problems that inspired them. Freud contended that dreams have both a manifest content and a latent content, the former being what dreams appear to be and the latter what they really are. In order to interpret dreams successfully, Freud argued that the psychologist has to be able to resolve the latent content of the dream so that the impulses driven by the id can surface. To help this process, Freud developed the technique of free association, which became one of the principal tools of psychoanalysis.

**Fantastic**
*Dreams are often fantastical and yet, to the dreamer, they seem entirely logical.*

### Free Association

**1** To free associate, pick any significant image or aspect of your dream. Keep it in your mind.

**2** What image or word comes to mind next? Keep the next image in your mind without analysing it in any way. What comes next? And next? And next? (For example, blue, lake, river, water, reflections, clouds, sky, bird, feather, boa, snake, bite, teeth, dentist, doctor, medicine...)

**3** Allow your mind to follow the string of images or ideas without judgment or interference. Keep going until you reach an image or idea that has a particular significance to you.

**4** If this does not happen, return to the initial dream image and begin again, or pick another image and start afresh.

### Preoccupations

Many dreams are so bizarre that they seem unfathomable, yet they are a reflection of the dreamer's waking life and preoccupations.

# Alfred Adler

**The superior man**
*Alfred Adler believed that dreams had the emotional power to solve dreamers' problems in their striving toward superiority.*

Alfred Adler (1870–1937) was born and trained in Vienna, practising as an ophthalmologist before turning to psychiatry and becoming one of the more prominent members of Freud's coterie. In 1911 he broke with his compatriot and began to study the psychology of the ego. He was an early feminist, firmly believing that society placed too much value on men and too little on women, and maintaining that the only viable relationship between the two sexes was one of equality.

## Community spirit

At the heart of Adler's theories was his overwhelmingly optimistic view of life. He believed that humans are capable of living together in harmony for the common good. He saw no contradiction between the individual and society, for he held that the more developed individuals are, the more they are able to communicate with society. In turn, the greater the degree of communication, the more the individual learns from society and therefore develops. This community spirit is not merely restricted to human relationships: according to Adler, it comprises all things, both animate and inanimate, until the individual is ultimately attuned to the universe.

## The inferiority complex

Adler held that all individuals are unique. He maintained that every aspect of the individual – emotional, mental, and physical – should be viewed in the light of the whole person, and not just as an isolated part. Adler proposed that individuals are not always ruled by reason, and may be guided by their unconscious belief of what is right, but that they ultimately strive towards achieving their full potential. He observed that individuals have the fundamental freedom to choose, but that they are often hampered by their own sense of power, or by their lack of it. He coined the phrases "superiority complex" and "inferiority complex" to describe these different states.

Unlike Freud, Adler claimed that dreams, and the experiences and emotions that are associated with them, can and should be brought into our waking lives. He believed that by interpreting and understanding our dreams we are able to identify and resolve our complexes.

## More Information

Adler can be considered to be an early proponent of psychosomatic and holistic medicine because he argued strongly in favour of the unity of mind and body.

**Childhood memories**

*A core technique that Adler pioneered to assess a client's lifestyle was the analysis of childhood memories and dreams.*

# ADLER ON THE INDIVIDUAL

Adler believed that because individuals behave as unified wholes, their dreams are consistent with their thoughts, emotions, memories, and actions. Each element may have its own idiosyncrasy, but because the guiding principle is the same, dreams speak volumes about a person's psychological or emotional problems. Adler believed that childhood memories – whether real or imagined – manifest the dreamer's key beliefs and emotions about himself and the world that he inhabits.

**Community care**

Adler encouraged role-play in groups. Other group members played the roles of parents, friends, lovers, or siblings, while Adler offered objective encouragement and realistic advice. Simultaneously, the client understood how to heal himself while the other group members increased their own community feeling by aiding and contributing to the development of another person.

### Role-play

In the middle stages of therapy Adler would advocate role-play. The client is encouraged to explore his identity, both actual and aspirational, examine missing emotions or experiences, and act out his new approach to them.

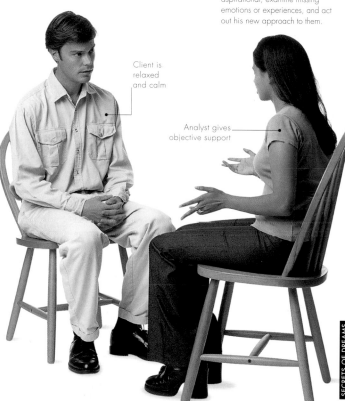

Client is relaxed and calm

Analyst gives objective support

# Carl Gustav Jung

**The enlightened dreamer**

*Jung maintained that dreams convey
to dreamers what they are ignoring or
are oblivious to in waking life.*

Carl Gustav Jung (1875–1961),
Freud's most influential
colleague in terms of
contemporary dream interpretation,
further extended the understanding and
research of dreams. Jung's fundamental
departure from Freudian theory was his
belief that the manifest nature of dreams
is a true representation of the inner
world of the dreamer. There is no latent
content that requires interpretation; all
that is needed is an understanding of
the symbolic games that the
unconscious mind plays when creating
a dream. But he also believed that
there is no reliable methodology for
interpreting dream symbols or imagery,
because every dream is unique in itself
and to the person who dreams it.

## A delicate balance

Jung maintained that it is imperative that
a dream should be discussed with the
dreamer, because only he or she has
the intuitive insight necessary to unravel
its underlying message. He firmly
believed that the chief function of
dreaming is to allow the unconscious
and conscious minds to reach a state
of balance and symmetry, so that the
issues that the dreamer has suppressed
or ignored can be brought to the
surface and made clear. He suspected
that dreams have the power to alter the
dreamer's future, in the sense that they
can reveal possibilities and choices.

## The collective unconscious

Where Jung differed radically from
Freud in his research on dream theory
was in his proposition of the theory of

archetypes and the collective unconscious. Like many of his predecessors, he felt that dreams are messages from a specific source, but could never quite identify whether that source is the dreamer or what he called the "collective unconscious". He defined the collective unconscious as being a shared pool of cultural memories, knowledge, and experience, to which each of us has access and which lies at the core of our psyche. Jung furthermore suggested that the collective unconscious contains what he called "archetypes". He described archetypes as being ideas or images that are common to all of us and that can be understood by everyone, regardless of their race, sex, or creed, because they contain a seminal truth that is universally applicable in our lives.

## More Information

Jung believed that we dream all the time, whether we are awake or asleep. He thought it likely that we dream continuously, but that our "noisy" consciousness swamps the dream.

**This is me**
*The self, the core of the personality, attracts all of the other archetypes and elements of the character, at both a conscious and unconscious level.*

# THE JUNGIAN ARCHETYPES

There are many Jungian archetypes that feature in dreams and convey a universal truth to us. Among the key archetypes that Jung identified are the persona, the shadow, the anima and animus, and the self.

**The shadow**
*The shadow symbolizes those darker aspects of ourselves that we do not like to acknowledge.*

### Anima/animus

*The anima and animus are qualities that are stereotypically linked to either the female (anima) or male (animus), such as gentleness, compassion or competitiveness and strength.*

### Archetypal Clues

There are a number of archetypes that are present in both masculine and feminine, and that have both a negative and positive aspect. The kind mother and father represent just, nurturing love while the destructive mother and ogre symbolize manipulation and despotism. The princess and the youth are spontaneous and carefree, the siren and the tramp are negative and self-absorbed. The priest and priestess are devoted to finding an essential truth and sharing it; the sorcerer and witch use their intuition for their own ends. But perhaps the most profound archetype is the mandala, for it represents the unity and faultlessness of the self. Each of us has our own mandala, and we strive to find it. Take note of the archetypes you see in your dreams and use them to illuminate your waking life.

### Society animal

*The persona is the face that we wear in society and represents the part of ourselves that we wish to reveal.*

# Fritz Perls

**Here and now**
*Perls reasoned that unless his clients were aware of themselves in the present they could not make sense of the past.*

Although Fritz Perls (1893–1970), a renowned German psychologist, was trained in traditional psychoanalytical techniques, his misgivings about certain Freudian theories led him to found what he called "Gestalt therapy".

## Gestalt therapy

The theory of Gestalt (the German word for "figure" or "form") argues that a person's inability to integrate all aspects of his or her personality into a healthy, fully functioning whole lies at the root of psychological or emotional disorders. The goal of Gestalt therapy is to teach people to recognize and acknowledge emotions and experiences, both within themselves and in their environment, so that they can respond with logic and precision to any situation.

## Dreams as microcosms

Perls broke with Freud and Jung in arguing that dream symbolism is not part of a universal symbolic language, but the personal creation of the individual who experiences the dream. He also differed from them in claiming that dream symbols should not be seen as instinctive drives, but rather as a projected part of the dreamer's personality at that given time. Perls firmly believed that dream interpretation should start with the premise that every character or object that crops up in a dream is a symbolic representation of some aspect of the dreamer's personality, known or unknown, and her experience of life. He argued, with logic, that since all dreamers are the architects of their own dreams, what appears in a dream must first be present in the dreamer.

## The empty chair

Perls used many different techniques to help his clients, including role-playing, asking questions of particular aspects of the self, and identifying opposites in the dream. He also developed the "empty chair" technique. In this technique, two chairs are placed opposite each other. The dreamer sits in one and talks to a person or object that was particularly significant in the dream before moving to the other chair and replying as he or she thinks that the person or object might do. This process of moving backwards and forwards between the two chairs, questioning and then responding, is repeated until the problem has been resolved.

### More Information

During the 1960s, Perls helped to establish many Gestalt-therapy centres in the United States, including Esalen in Big Sur, California.

**The empty chair**
*This technique allows you to explore your dream by talking to a significant dream symbol and then answering for it.*

# ANN FARADAY

The dream researcher Ann Faraday makes no secret of her debt to Gestalt. She suggests using either Perls's empty-chair technique or the "top-dog–underdog" technique in level three of her dream-interpretation technique. (The top-dog–underdog technique encourages dreamers to identify the part of their personality – the top dog – that considers itself superior to, and is often judgmental of, the oppressed part – the underdog – which always means well, but never quite succeeds.) Faraday believes that dreams have three different levels of meaning, and that it is vital to identify and understand all three.

**Leader of the pack**
*The top-dog–underdog technique allows you to identify the core extremes of your personality.*

## A Looking-Glass World

### LEVEL ONE
The first level encourages you to look outwards from your dream and to take note of any external events that you did not consciously address while you were awake. Faraday contends that the meaning of your dream is often direct, and reminds or warns you of impending problems.

### LEVEL TWO
The second level explores your unique perception of the world. Borrowing from the author Lewis Carroll, Faraday calls this the "looking-glass self". By interpreting dream characters, animals, buildings, the weather, and so on, she maintains that you can decipher who you really are and your relationship with the world around you.

### LEVEL THREE
Level three asks you to look inward to identify the conflict within yourself, as well as your will and ability to resolve it. Faraday asserts that by using some of the Gestalt techniques to explore the core problem, the existential message of your dream will often unfold. If so, you will ultimately confront and resolve the four key existential life issues, which are as follows:
- nothing lasts
- we are all eventually alone
- life is meaningless
- we all die

**Adrift**

*The dream setting seems particularly significant in this 1886 artwork as the boat approaches the entrance to a shadowy land.*

# Medard Boss

**Restricted**

*Boss believed that if we are worried about something we will dream of being restricted or trapped.*

Medard Boss (1903–90), a Swiss psychotherapist, was influenced by Freudian theories until 1938, when he became associated with Jung, who opened up to him the possibilities of other forms of psychoanalysis. It was his fascination with the works of Ludwig Binswanger and Martin Heidegger, however, and his eventual friendship with Heidegger, that led him inexorably towards the theories of existential psychology. He is often thought of as its co-founder.

## Gelassenheit

Existential psychology is based on the idea that we each choose what we wish to be and then express this choice in everything that we do. Boss rejected the Freudian and Jungian beliefs that dreams have manifest or latent content, and also his fellow existentialist Binswanger's ideas that there is a world design. He felt that the idea that people enter this world with innate expectations and archetypes detracts from the primary principles of existentialism: that the world reveals itself and is not something to be interpreted, while human existence is shared existence, and we illuminate ourselves and each other in everything that we do. One of Boss's most important instructions to his clients was the need for *Gelassenheit* (the German word for composure, which is often interpreted as "letting go"). He believed that although most of us button ourselves up and stifle our own lives because we desire always to be in control, we should take a leap of faith and trust in life itself.

## The real truth

Boss was fascinated by dreams and considered them a very important part of therapy. He did not see them as symbolic, however, but as portraits of how dreamers illuminate their own lives. Wish-fulfilment in a dream is therefore highly significant, according to Boss, and may be patently obvious. If we feel liberated, for example, we will fly in our dreams, while if we are worried or frightened about something or someone, we may dream of being chased or trapped. Boss suggested that dreamers should allow dreams to reveal themselves to them, arguing that if they saw the images before them plainly and properly, they would soon understand their own existential condition and, as a result, also comprehend what was wrong or right with it.

### More Information

Medard Boss graduated from Zurich University in 1928 and then studied further in Paris and Vienna, where he was himself analysed by Sigmund Freud.

**Precision engineering**
*Boss believed that if dreamers tried too hard to analyse what their dream symbols meant it would inhibit them from grasping the core truth of the dream.*

# DREAMS AS MIRRORS

Medard Boss always began his dream work with the dreamer's "explication". This might at first be a sketchy account of the dream, which Boss then encouraged the client to elaborate upon. Boss discouraged free association or amplification, which he felt led away from the existential message of the dream. Instead, Boss asked his clients to stay as close as possible to the dream symbols, to describe them in detail and their reactions to them.

**1 Machine dreams**
*One of Medard Boss's most famous examples of dream interpretation was an engineer who was sexually repressed, lonely, and downhearted. In the initial stages of his dream therapy, the engineer dreamed only of the machinery that surrounded him in his everyday work, but his dreams gradually began to change as he continued his therapy. He slowly began to dream of living, rather than inanimate, things.*

## 2 Birds and bees

*First he dreamed of plants, then of insects, then of frogs, snakes, mice, rabbits, and pigs. Finally, two years into his therapy, he began to dream of women. Boss concluded that because the man had identified himself with his work to the exclusion of all else, it had taken him this amount of time to dream of the one thing that he really did want to share his life with. The man's solitary nature, depression, and malaise were the result of his having hidden himself from the world behind his machinery*

## 3 A true reflection

*What is striking to note in Boss's work is that he does not ascribe any symbolism to the images that appear in the engineer's dreams, instead allowing the dreams to speak for themselves. Thus Boss does not interpret the snake as a sexual image (as Freud would have done) and does not identify the pig with an archetype or complex. The images that the engineer conjures up in his sleeping mind are both unique to himself and the images that illuminate his life at that particular moment.*

# Dreaming in Other Cultures

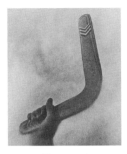

**Attunement**

*With skill, a boomerang returns to its owner; with acute sensitivity, Aborigines can contact their ancestor spirits.*

There are a number of other cultural approaches to dreams, such as those of the Aborigines of Australia, the Senoi of Malaysia, and the Native American peoples.

## The Dreamtime

The Aborigines' concept of dreaming is quite unique, because they believe that the universe was created during the "Dreamtime". For the Aborigines, everything in our world holds a vibration, whose echoes tell of the circumstances and the ancestor spirits that created it. The power of a place – its sacredness – is therefore linked to the ancestor spirits, holding a memory of those spirits known as the "Dreaming". Only in moments of extraordinary attunement can one be aware of the dreaming of the earth. Nevertheless, the ancestor spirits are present in the forms into which they changed at the end of the Dreamtime, now and in the future.

## The Senoi

Until recently, our understanding of the western Senoi dream theory was based on the erroneous belief that the Senoi people controlled their dreams to promote their emotional health, and that dreams were analysed and discussed every morning, with adults advising children on their dream behaviour and reactions. Ann Faraday and John Wren Lewis recently travelled to Malaysia, however, and discovered that although the Senoi people frequently dance or go into trance sessions in which dream-inspired songs are used to call the spirits, they would not consider manipulating dreams to serve their own purposes. In fact, they believe that it is the *gunig*, or protective spirit, that chooses the human vehicle for enlightenment. They pay close attention if anyone receives a song or a dance in their dreams, for it signifies the emergence of a new shaman, who will interpret dreams as omens or warnings and will invoke protective spirits.

## The Native Americans

The Native American peoples believe that dreams serve many purposes: they are a means of divining the future, of contacting supernatural spirit guides, as well as of resolving emotional or psychological problems. Different tribes use different means to incubate and interpret dreams: the Iroquois, for example, hold festivals at which they dance and "perform" their dreams. Common to all tribes, however, is the belief that if you wish for a dream to give you specific guidance, it will be given to you by your spirit guide.

# KINDS OF DREAM

Betty Bethards, author of *The Dream Book*, maintains that there are six basic kinds of dream. ✍ The clearing-house dream. ✍ The insight, or teaching, dream. ✍ The problem-solving dream – a dream that you actively seek. ✍ The precognitive dream, which gives you a glimpse of the future and alerts you to the possibilities that may ensue. ✍ The prophetic dream, which comes from the very highest level of expanded consciousness and concerns spiritual growth. ✍ The "outside-interference" dream, which is generated by something in your external environment.

# The Debris-clearing and Trash-can Theory

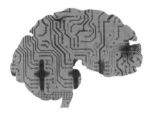

**Computer brain**
*Some scientists believe dreams represent the systematic programme clearance of a sophisticated computer – the brain.*

While most dream analysts believe that dreams are tools for psychological development, there are some scientists who believe that they are nothing more than the systematic clearing out of your brain's memory bank.

The British computer analysts Christopher Evans and Ted Newman draw a parallel between the brain and a computer, in that both contain, sort, and file vast quantities of data. They maintain that all levels of sleep (but REM sleep in particular) occur when the conscious brain is switched off and dissociated from the body. During this time the brain is able to open up its memory banks and to re-organize the huge quantity of material contained in the neural network that is pertinent to events experienced during the day. They explain the fact that you may be able to remember your dreams by classifying dreams as type A and type B. Type A represents the full reprogramming that occurs while you are asleep, while type B is a fragment of the type A dream, which we remember on gaining consciousness.

## Taking out the trash

Building on Evans and Newman's work, in 1947 Francis Crick set out to explain two conundrums: the mystery of life and the mystery of consciousness. He and his colleague James Watson solved the first, by discovering the double-helix structure of DNA, for which they shared the Nobel prize for medicine. To try to explain the second, in 1983 Crick hypothesized that all of our emotions, memories, and drives are simply the workings of a vast neural network. Along with his colleague Graeme Mitchison he began to study dreams because he wanted to comprehend how groups of neurons interact. He discovered that neural nets do not store memories logically, instead dropping one on top of the other if too many are introduced. While searching for a device that would re-organize these jumbled memories, it struck the two men that perhaps this occurred during REM sleep. Crick calls this process "unlearning", or "reverse learning", which is distinct from forgetting because it is the brain's means of selecting, and dispensing with, useless information.

## More Information

Crick feels that it is not beneficial to remember your dreams, since they represent the very information that your brain is trying to excise.

**The cryptic clue**
*Like many others before and since, Friedrich August Kekulé (1829–96) unravelled a conundrum by heeding his dreams.*

# PROBLEM-SOLVING
Problem-solving is an approach diametrically opposed to Crick and Mitchison's dream theory. Even if you do not intentionally use your dreams to solve a conundrum, you may have experienced sleeping on a problem and waking up the next morning with a solution. Betty Bethards will tell you that you should be deeply relaxed when programming your mind to receive a problem-solving dream, and that you should never be discouraged if the dream's message is unclear. You should also note that you need to ask your question with integrity and proper intent. This is because you should be asking a question to gain insight into yourself rather than using it to manipulate events or other people. You may ask the wrong question or request an answer that you do not really want to know, but you should always be honest when asking for a problem-solving dream.

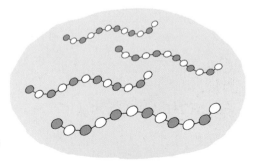

**Snakes alive**
*In trying to construct a benzene molecule Kekulé could not find a way of arranging the six carbon and six hydrogen atoms in a conventional chain.*

### Friedrich August Kekulé

There are numerous examples of the problem-solving dream, many of which fall into the realm of creative science because they have helped to put the pieces of a puzzle together. One of the most famous is Friedrich August Kekulé's dream. Kekulé, a German chemist who had been struggling to discover the molecular structure of benzene, claimed that the answer came to him in a dream. He dreamed that he saw numerous molecules dancing before his eyes, some large, some small. Although some of the smaller ones would pair off and be surrounded by a larger one from time to time, the whole structure kept revolving in a snakelike motion. Suddenly Kekulé saw one of these "snakes" grab its own tail. Waking instantly, he recognized the significance of the imagery: benzene's molecular structure was, in fact, a ring.

**Eureka**
*The benzene molecule revealed itself to Kekulé in all its simplicity.*

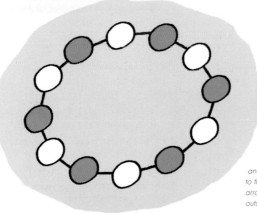

**Snake bite**
*By arranging the carbon atoms in a ring, each atom could share bonds with its neighbouring atom, while allowing another bond to attach to the hydrogen atoms arranged around the outside of the ring.*

# Teaching Dreams

**Physical readings**
*Of more than 14,000 recorded readings by Cayce, around two-thirds were for people who had health problems.*

Teaching dreams are distinct from problem-solving dreams, in that they are not dreams that you ask for but dreams that are given to you, either from a higher dimension or from the deepest core of your own latent awareness. These dreams bring to the forefront snatches of intuition that you have experienced during the day, allowing you to see the essential truth of a situation or relationship. The fact that your dreaming mind is prompting you to remember suggests that you need to acknowledge a principle that your conscious mind has rejected or chosen to ignore. You will probably receive at least one important teaching dream each night, maybe more.

## The sleeping prophet

The American psychic Edgar Cayce (1877–1945) found that his dreams gave him astonishing insights into the human condition. For more than forty years he gave what he called "psychic readings". He developed the ability to give these readings by putting himself into a dream-like trance. In this self-generated, altered state of awareness, he seemed to have access to an incredible fund of universal knowledge, and could answer any question that was put to him.

Cayce discovered his unique gift by accident, when he lost his voice and his doctors seemed to be unable to help him. Following a friend's suggestion that he consult his own subconscious through hypnosis, he learned that he could diagnose his own problems, as well as other people's. While lying down, he would put himself into a trance and would then respond to any questions that were asked of him with astonishing accuracy and perspicacity. Although he never remembered what he had said in his trances, his words were recorded as he spoke.

People came to him for diagnoses of illnesses that could not be identified by the medical community. Cayce was not only able to diagnose their illnesses in his trance-like state, but also prescribed treatments that could alleviate the problem. He sometimes noticed karmic problems that had a bearing upon the ailment, and began to receive requests for life-readings. In any life-reading that he gave, Cayce was scrupulous in identifying only those past experiences that were appropriate to the life that his client was leading at that time.

### More Information

Cayce made over 30,000 diagnoses with absolute accuracy, but never used his gift for fame or fortune, instead using it to treat sick people or to give spiritual advice.

**Shipwreck**
Many people, including the author Graham Greene, claim to have foreseen the sinking of the Titanic.

# PRECOGNITION OR PROPHECY?

A precognitive dream gives you a glimpse of the future and alerts you to the possibilities that may ensue. Betty Bethards distinguishes it from *déjà vu* by pointing out that precognition usually involves dreaming of someone other than yourself. Whether these dreams are the result of intuitive guesswork is still a matter worthy of debate. She suggests that if you have a precognitive dream it is probably designed to awaken you to the possibilities of the mind and to develop your desire to learn more about your inner self.

**A shaft of light**
A prophetic dream is one that Bethards believes comes from the highest level of expanded awareness and concerns spiritual growth. This dream has many of the qualities of a lucid dream: you are aware that you are not awake, yet at the same time you know that you are dreaming. Bethards maintains that if you have a prophetic dream it will be on a grand scale, and will encompass an insight and understanding of the unity of all life.

## Disturbed Dreams

Bethards claims that a dream can be generated by what she calls "outside interference". This can be caused by anything in your physical environment that disturbs you sufficiently to cause you to incorporate it into your dream. You may hear the phone ringing or a dog barking when they really are, for example, or you may feel icy cold and wake up to find that your bedclothes have fallen off. When interpreting a dream, Bethards points out that you must take into consideration the possibility that outside interference may have altered the scope of your dream.

**Answer the phone**
*Sometimes you will incorporate noises, such as a ringing phone, or changes in temperature in your external environment, into your dream.*

# Questions and Answers

**Dream recall**
*According to research, you forget as much as 95 per cent of your dreams.*

A number of questions are frequently asked about dreams. The most common queries are posed and answered here to elucidate or expand upon the theories examined in the preceding chapters.

**Q** *Do people dream in black and white?*
**A** Since colour represents a pre-eminent part of our lives, it is likely that we dream in colour more often than not, even if we do not remember the colours. But instances of black-and-white dreaming have been recorded.

**Q** *How long does a dream last?*
**A** Dream time lasts as long as it would take you to imagine the narrative in real time. This may seem strange, since the dream packs an enormous amount of information into what appears to be just seconds. The dream achieves this by concentrating on key incidents or characters and cutting swiftly from one situation to another. Dreams have been recorded that have lasted as long as 45 minutes.

**Q** *Do dreams come true?*
**A** Some people believe that dreams are presentiments of future events, often disastrous ones. In most cases, however, they simply contain shafts of intuition that our conscious minds have buried, which, when brought to light, illuminate, and therefore verify, our waking experience.

**Q** *Will I dream less as I grow older?*
**A** Probably not, although it is difficult to generalize. Babies certainly spend a great deal of time in REM sleep, but

REM sleep in adults maintains a fairly steady pattern well into old age. It is possible that, while older people do dream, they do not remember having done so.

**Q** *When am I most likely to remember my dreams?*
**A** Just before waking, when the longest period of REM sleep occurs. You may also remember elements of an earlier dream if you woke up shortly after going to sleep.

**Q** *Do animals dream?*
**A** There is no evidence to prove that they do, but if you are a dog-owner you'll probably testify to the fact that they appear to, since they go through all of the physiological changes that a human does while sleeping.

**Q** *Does a heavy meal affect sleep?*
**A** Yes. It is inevitable if you eat and drink heartily before going to bed that your digestive system will suffer and a restless night will ensue.

# DREAM WORK

Rosemary Ellen Guiley, author of *Dreamwork for the Soul*, believes that dreams are the richest source of spiritual guidance and emotional or physical healing. Once you have learned how to interpret dreams and the wisdom they convey, you can use them for your own growth and fulfilment. She warns, however, that a dream can only truly heal if you act on the knowledge it imparts. If you learn how to remember and record your dreams you will gain extraordinary insights into yourself, others, and life itself. Dream working should be a regular ritual, working alone or in a group. Group settings are helpful as they offer objective insights that you might not have arrived at alone.

# Recalling Your Dreams

**Stay still**
*Move as little as possible on waking and hold the dream in your head so that you can record it.*

Those people who say they never dream are mistaken. We all dream but some of us remember and some do not. It is simply a matter of training yourself to recall your dream of the night before. With practice and the right technique, you will soon learn how to remember one or even several of the dreams you have. Erratic or fitful sleep will inhibit dreaming. Check first that there are no underlying health problems that could influence your sleep pattern. It is also possible that alcohol or drugs may hinder your capacity to dream.

### The dream journal

The most important factor in recalling your dreams is your will to do so. In order to help you fulfil this aim, all dream analysts recommend that you keep a record of all your dreams. They suggest either the use of a notebook for that specific purpose, or a tape recorder so that you can verbally record your impressions of a dream. If you do not understand a message in a dream, do not worry; you will have one or more further dreams that teach you the same message until you can grasp the core meaning. It is particularly important that you make a mental note of any emotions that you felt in the dream and immediately upon waking. You will discover that these feelings are vital to the interpretation of the dream since they provide the clue to its meaning.

### Personal development

Keeping a dream journal will make it easier to interpret your dreams. By dating the entries in your dream journal you can see how recurring or similar dreams evolve and develop, and your perception of yourself and others will deepen. Recording dreams can also show you obvious behavioural patterns that are hindering your spiritual and emotional development. By bringing into the open your innermost thoughts and wishes, you will be able to discern what motivates and drives you in life.

Lori Reid, astrologer, palmist, and dream analyst, recommends that if you wake during a dream, or if the dream has been distressing, you should remain still and silent and try to return to the dream. By using visualization, you can change the scope of the action so that your dream has a more positive and satisfactory conclusion.

### Did you Know?

Dream analyst Lori Reid maintains that remembering your dreams is as simple as ABC. Ask yourself a question. Before you go to bed repeat it to yourself. Concentrate on the question. If you tell yourself that you are going to recall your dream and get the answer, you probably will.

**Getting it down**
*It is important to write down or record everything you can remember from your dream on waking, before you forget it.*

# RECORDING YOUR DREAMS

David Fontana, Fellow of the British Psychological Society, states that you should first come to dream interpretation with the belief that your dreams hold personal messages. He also warns that although you may not succeed at first, you should persist, because your dream journal will be a rewarding tool for self-analysis and personal growth. He suggests that you try setting your alarm clock to go off during the second period of REM sleep, approximately three hours after you have gone to sleep, because you are then likely to wake up in the middle of a dream. If you are not successful, you could try setting the alarm a few minutes sooner or later, until you find a time that coincides with a dream.

**Sleep with intent**
*If you wish to remember a dream then go to bed with the clear intention to do so.*

## Dream Journal

**1** During the day, remind yourself that you wish to remember your dream.

**2** Place your dream journal or tape recorder beside your bed and record the date.

**3** When you go to bed, sit quietly on the side of the bed and relax. Now tell yourself that you want to remember your dream and that you will remember it.

**4** On waking, lie still and concentrate on the thoughts and emotions that are running through your head, as well as the contents of your dream.

## Be exact

Be sure to get down as much detail as possible – the setting and any important emotions, actions, or characters.

**5** Write down or record these details as quickly as you can. Your comments should be precise and comprehensive, and the sequence of events should be given in their proper order. Use the present tense to make the dream experience both relevant and immediate.

**6** Take particular note of dream characters and environments. Do you associate them with anyone or anywhere in particular? If so, note this down.

**7** Record any famous people that appeared in your dream and how they differed from the real person. Make a note of any magical or mythical creatures and colours, too.

**8** Do any events, characters, or motifs recur? If so, do they always do so in the same way? Make a note of these details.

**9** Record your emotional responses to everything.

**10** Re-examine your dream emotions and actions throughout the following day.

JULY 12

One night I dreamt of flying above
meadows on a summer evening. I am
flying standing up, my arms outstretched.
A man comes along side me, flying
horizontally and asks me why I'm flying
up right, why not horizontally like everyone
else? I reply that I'm happy flying the
way I do. It works for me!

# Dream Work in Groups

**Group therapy**
*Sharing dreams in groups allows
other members of the group to illuminate
a particular problem for the dreamer.*

Although Fritz Perls (see pages
56–57) was one of the first
people to introduce the idea of
dreamers interpreting their own dreams,
he also encouraged clients to explore
their dreams in groups. His reasoning
behind this was that other members of
the group could often illuminate a
particular problem better than the
dreamer. At the same time, however,
he insisted that the dream was the
intellectual property of the dreamer,
and that he should not have any
interpretation imposed upon him.

## Montague Ullman

Since the work of Perls, the most
significant contribution to the field of
dream work in the community has been
the research conducted by Montague
Ullman, the founder in New York City
in 1961 of one of the first sleep
laboratories devoted to the study of
dreams and telepathy. Ullman, a life
fellow of the American Psychiatric
Association, has remained tireless in
encouraging the development of dream-
sharing groups in the USA and
Sweden. The Dream Group Forum, a
Swedish association, is today devoted
to training others in Ullman's methods.

## A social awareness

Ullman maintains that a dream is a
social phenomenon, even more so
when it is shared with a group. Dreams
shared with others, Ullman believes,
can speak volumes about people's
place in society and their adaptability
to it. Sharing dreams can raise
emotional, social, political, and cultural
awareness in all of the participants,

but particularly in the dreamer. Using subtle questioning, other group members can lead the dreamer to greater self-analysis. It is not the job of the other workers to interpret the dreamer's dream messages, however, but to encourage him to examine each facet of the dream. By being offered insights in a non-confrontational way, the dreamer can absorb difficult emotional traumas and recognize the core problem more clearly.

## Cyberspace

In more recent years, dream work has been carried out in cyberspace. Jeremy Taylor, a Unitarian Universalist minister and former president of the Association for the Study of Dreams, is one of the key dream researchers engaged in such work. One of the advantages of this form of dream work is that it can be conducted across time and geographical barriers. The anonymity of cyberspace also allows all of the participants to contribute to dream work unhampered by common prejudices.

**Tossing and turning**

*While many of us move a great deal in bed while sleeping, when we dream we are usually very still.*

# DREAM-SHARING

If you wish to set up your own dream-work group, you could do no better than to follow Montague Ullman's blueprint. Once you have described your dream, the other members of your group should each make mental connections of their own, as if the dream were theirs. The other members should each talk about the sensations that they experienced when hearing about the dream, but without implying that you, the dreamer, should think or feel the same. You can then select from the group's observations whatever feels informative and right.

## Setting Up a Group

Jeremy Taylor believes that dream-sharing groups can become the basis for truly profound psychospiritual experiences. His toolkit for dream work advises you to remember six points.

**1** We dream to achieve wholeness and well-being.

**2** Our dreams are multifaceted.

**3** Our dreams give us a new awareness and do not go over old ground.

**4** Only the dreamer can recognize the language and truly interpret her dream.

**5** If you are talking to the dreamer about her dream, talk about it as if it were your own and you were interpreting it for yourself.

**6** All group dream-workers should agree to maintain confidentiality.

### A rich tapestry

*Each dream is unique to the dreamer and only
she can translate its language and symbolism.
Other group members bring their own insight
which the dreamer can use or reject.*

# Dream Interpretation

**Free association**
*From apple to tree to fire,
free association can take you
on an intriguing journey.*

As we have seen, there are many ways in which to interpret dreams, either working on your own or as part of a group. Freud, who believed that dreams reveal the darker side of human nature, set out to explore and interpret the latent content of dreams by means of free association. If you practise free association, it will almost certainly reveal an affinity with higher wisdom, enabling you to recognize an essential truth that you may, in fact, already know, but have buried deep within your psyche. Free association will bring this truth to your conscious notice.

## Amplification

Jung, on the other hand, argued that you dream in order to integrate every aspect of the psyche, and that free association muddies the waters by diverting you from a dream's true meaning. In other words, although you will find it a unique tool for learning something meaningful about yourself, what you learn as a result may well be different from what your dream was really trying to convey.

Jung instead chose to use the amplification method. Rather than seeking the hidden meaning within a dream, this technique asks you to describe each dream symbol, explain what it means to you and then connect it with your waking life. Much like free association, you select a symbol, examine it from every aspect and note what this information sparks off. What is the next image that you visualize? Look at the new image from every angle, but do not allow yourself to make another association and keep the initial image firmly in your mind.

Rather than building up associations that will lead you away from your dream, you are building multiple levels of meaning around a central image.

## The world's a stage

Perls's role-playing technique is interesting because it allows you to explore every facet of your dream, including the images that you found particularly pertinent and those that you barely registered. For Perls, no aspect of the dream is insignificant: the fact that you overlooked, or virtually ignored, an image or object may mean that it has something important to tell you.

Today's dream analysts are perhaps less exclusive in their methods of dream interpretation, borrowing as they do from Jung, Gestalt, existentialism, and sometimes also Freud in order to elucidate dreams.

### More Information

You will probably find that your dreams come in cycles. You will recall some with ease and will find others difficult to remember.

# THE DREAM INTERVIEW

Co-founder of the Delaney and Flowers Dream Center, and founding president of the International Association for the Study of Dreams, Gayle Delaney has been pivotal in pioneering and popularizing dream research. With Jan Edelstein, she runs corporate training programmes that offer employees the opportunity to learn how to raise their productivity and reduce accidents and illness through good sleeping habits.

## Talk it through

*Firmly believing that dreams contain messages that are pertinent to any salient issues in the dreamer's life, Delaney has created the dream-interview method of interpretation.*

## Technique

*1 Begin by dream-diagramming. This entails writing down your dream and highlighting its key elements using a specific code. Circle the main characters (both people and animals), underline each major object, draw a wavy line around any feelings or emotions, highlight all settings with a rectangle and put an arrow below any important actions.*

I'm back in childhood again. I'm a little girl. I'm running through a forest. I'm being chased by a wolf. I keep looking behind me because I'm sure I can feel the wolf's breath on my neck. I'm terrified.

**2** *Start the interview. Retell the dream in the first person and in the present tense. The listener then asks you five questions about your dream.*
- *"What environment do you inhabit?"*
- *"Who are the characters?"*
- *"What events occur?"*
- *"What objects appear?"*
- *"What emotions do you experience?"*

*After each question, the listener asks you if you can draw a link between your dream world and your waking life.*

**3** *After examining the dream from every angle, the listener retells the dream to you, bearing in mind all that she has been told and on the basis of what she has gleaned from your answers to her questions. This should result in what Jeremy Taylor calls the "A-ha" factor: the dawning light of recognition and expanded awareness.*

**4** *The listener then asks you one final question: "What is your understanding of this dream?", that is, "What does it mean?"*

### A trusted ear
*It is vital that the dreamer is with an interviewer that she feels she can trust.*

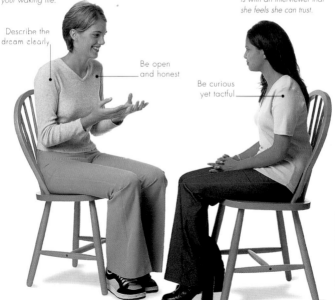

Describe the dream clearly

Be open and honest

Be curious yet tactful

# Clinical Dream Research

**Negative to positive**
*Barry Krakow has pioneered a method to help victims of trauma transform disturbing dreams to positive ones.*

Recent research has shown that dreams can be a clear indication of post-traumatic stress disorder. If you have suffered a serious trauma, such as a near-death experience or the sudden loss of a loved one in abnormal circumstances, you will often replay the sequence of events over and over again in your dreams, not just night after night, but often several times a night. These dreams can then become highly traumatic themselves for those who suffer from this syndrome.

## Sleep disorders

Barry Krakow, the founder of the Nightmare Treatment Center in New Mexico and a pioneer in the treatment of chronic nightmares and disturbing dreams, has done a great deal of research in this area. Krakow's main expertise is working with people who suffer from nightmares, insomnia, or post-traumatic stress disorder.

In a study of 598 women who attended a rape crisis centre, 82 per cent were rape victims and the other 18 per cent were victims of sexual assault. The rape victims reported a significantly higher proportion of nightmares than those who had been sexually assaulted, but not raped. Of the rape victims, 26 per cent reported a lot of nightmares and 53 per cent some nightmares; of the victims of sexual assault, 21 per cent reported many nightmares and 45 per cent a few. Krakow concluded that although the nightmares were unrelated to the rape or assaults on these women, their change in sleeping habits had a direct correlation to the preponderance of traumatic dreams. In a paper published in *Comprehensive Psychiatry*, Krakow theorized that the self-reported evidence of the dreams of 150 sexual-assault victims suggested that more than 50 per cent suffered from sleep apnoea (a temporary inability to breathe).

## Imagery-rehearsal treatment

Krakow has developed this technique to help people who have recurring nightmares resulting from trauma. While they are awake, Krakow asks them to recall details of their nightmares, and to replace the negative images with positive ones. As part of a group of dream-workers, they build new dreams on the foundations of the old ones and then practise the positive dreams until they have replaced the nightmares.

### More Information

During withdrawal, alcoholics and drug abusers often find that they have aggressive and unpleasant nightmares. Withdrawal dreams are characteristically full of self-loathing and violence.

# DREAM THEMES

In order to understand your dreams, it is important that you learn more about the common themes that run through dreams, regardless of your race, culture, or social history. As Betty Bethards puts it, dreams help you to discover your true potential and to see yourself as you truly are. As she says, the single most difficult obstacle to self-awareness is your own unwillingness to use the tools you are given. Both dreams and meditation teach you valuable life lessons. Waking life provides you with the opportunity to practise what you have learned.

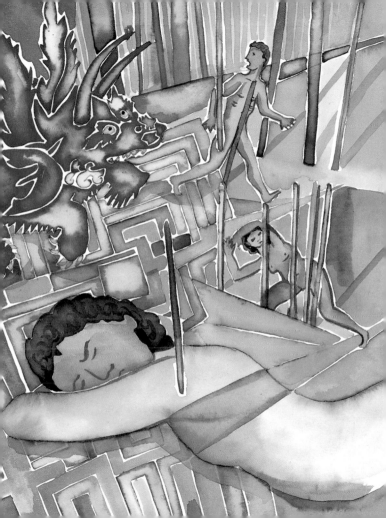

# The Cycle of Life

**Wishful thinking**
*If you are longing to conceive, a birth dream might be a message from your inner self that you are pregnant.*

Dreams of birth and death are common. Symbolically rich, they often occur at key moments in your life when transformation is about to occur. They signify the end of one cycle and the beginning of the next.

## Birth

Unsurprisingly, birth dreams are more common in women than in men. Women often dream of birth or labour as an unconscious way of preparing themselves for the real thing. Both Betty Bethards and Lori Reid suggest that if

you are longing to conceive, dreaming of a birth may be a message from your inner self that you wish to do so. Men may dream of a birth or labour for reasons of anxiety, often reporting that, as fathers, they feel that they will be excluded when the baby arrives.

Birth dreams are predominantly associated with new beginnings, however. Men, in particular, equate this dream with the start of a new business venture or creative idea, while women may link it to more psychological concerns, such as a relationship or a new awareness. If you dream of observing a birth, your dream may either be inviting you to assist in someone else's transformation or may reflect your concern for their well-being.

## Death

Dreams of death are always disturbing, particularly when they concern the death of a parent or lover. There is conflicting opinion about this kind of dream. Jung would suggest that you were trying symbolically to sever emotional ties. The Jungian analyst Jeremy Taylor says that although every dream invites you to adopt new understandings and insights, death is the single most frequent universal image of spiritual growth. In his opinion, it does not matter who, or what, dies, for any such dream signifies significant development, but the way in which the death occurs may indicate the depth of your desire to change. If you die in your dream, the changes may be fundamental; if someone else dies, the changes are likely to be more subtle; if you commit suicide, the change is due to a conscious choice. However, Gayle Delaney believes that death dreams do not herald the end of one lifestyle and the beginning of another, but symbolize some aspect of your life that is fundamentally wrong.

### More Information

David Fontana suggests that if you are sure that someone who has died has communicated with you in a dream, this may very well be the case.

**Senior management**

*David is managing director of his father's firm – a significant achievement for one so young.*

# THE COFFIN

David dreams that he witnesses the birth of a baby boy and watches this child grow up. At first, it seems to David that the child is his father, but it gradually dawns on him that the child is himself. He watches him excel at artistic and creative pursuits, particularly woodwork and carpentry, then change direction and study for a business degree, before joining the family firm. After that he sees his own funeral and is conscious of many faceless people mourning him. He hears several of them say, "What a tragedy! He was so talented and so young." He walks up to the coffin and sees his own corpse lying there. As he stops to look, the corpse opens its eyes and simply says "change".

David's creative genius is stifled by his sense of loyalty and duty and he puts his energy into his father's business.

## Dream Analysis

Most analysts view dreams of birth and death as being symbolic of change. The death dream indicates the need to bury the past and move on to a new way of thinking or a greater awareness. In *The Dream Game*, Ann Faraday insists that if you dream of your own death it symbolizes the need to transcend an old self-image.

David used the empty-chair technique to analyse this dream for himself. He quickly came to the conclusion that the dream was displaying all of his frustrations at being forced along a path that he did not really want to take. He had studied for his degree and had entered the family business because his father wished it, rather than following his own ambition, which was to become a cabinetmaker. He realized that he was literally dying inside: his creative bent was being stifled in an attempt to please others.

David realizes that in order to feel truly fulfilled he must follow his own dream.

# Anxiety Dreams

**Victimized**
*If you cannot connect your attack dream with waking life, you may have some ongoing emotional problem.*

There are a number of dreams that could be classed as anxiety dreams. Among the most common are dreams of being chased, of being attacked, trapped, or lost. They all show different atavistic fears, or deep-seated problems, that you may be suppressing or unwilling to address.

## The chase

The overwhelming emotion in dreams of being chased is fear and helplessness: you run as fast as your legs can carry you to get away from your pursuer, but your feet feel as though they were stuck in cement. It is important to consider how the pursuit evolved. Did you manage to get away, or did your pursuer begin to gain on you? Did you have the courage to turn and face your pursuer? If you were able to do this, your fear will often evaporate, as will the hunter and the dream.

Jeremy Taylor insists that this dream is symbolic of inner prompts to let go of unnecessary notions or emotions in order to develop. Such dreams often become recurring dreams if you have not recognized what you are fearful of or are unwilling to change.

## Feeling trapped

It is not difficult to draw a parallel between waking life and dream life when you dream that you are caged or trapped. What do you find frustrating in your life? What is holding you back? Do you feel unable to shoulder your responsibilities? Do you feel that you have had burdens thrust upon you that are beyond you? Is your personal freedom being threatened? Or are you being hampered by your own lack of self-confidence? Identify the source of your unease and the dream will stop.

## Under attack

Attack dreams often turn into chase dreams because your instinctive response to an attack is to run. Your attacker may appear in a multitude of forms: as a monster, another person, a wild animal, or a mythical creature.

You may not have to look far to identify your "assailant". Is there some kind of unresolved conflict with another person in your waking life, most probably in your workplace? If you are unable to identify aggression in those around you, look at your inner world: are you punishing yourself because of an unresolved internal struggle?

### More Information

Calvin Hall, who has done extensive research on attack dreams, has discovered that if the assailant is human rather than animal, male aggressors are overwhelmingly implicated.

**Self-doubt**
*Harry has all the tools for success at his disposal if only he trusted his own judgment.*

# I'M LOST
Harry finds himself in a vast, dark, subterranean cavern. Although he knows that he has never been here before, he also knows that he should be able to find the way out. He spins around and around, trying to make sense of where he is, but in doing so loses all sense of direction and realizes that he is hopelessly lost. He notices that tiny shafts of light seem to be filtering down to him from several directions, but does not know which will give him the clue to the route that leads to the surface. Feeling frightened and helpless, he collapses on the ground, utterly defeated.

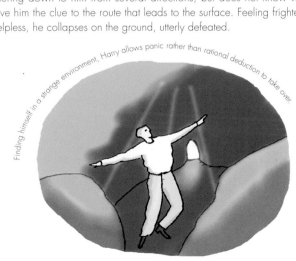

Finding himself in a strange environment, Harry allows panic rather than rational deduction to take over.

## Dream Analysis

Dreaming of being lost parallels a loss of direction or purpose in your waking life. You may be feeling insecure and unsure of yourself, and may believe you lack the ability or motivation to be decisive. The Jungian interpretation would suggest that the dream has stripped away your social veneer, your persona, to reveal what you are feeling at the deepest level. Jeremy Taylor contends that if you are able to link your feelings of being lost in your dream with your waking life, you may discover where you think you have lost your grip. By asking yourself penetrating questions, you could solve the problem.

In Harry's case, the environment in which his dream takes place is significant. Caves are associated with the unconscious mind, with the unexplored parts of the self. It is also significant that he spins around and around in his search for the exit. He is almost willing himself to become confused, while still instinctively knowing that he can still find the way out of the cave. In a dream, light always signifies enlightenment, so the shafts of light in his dream are telling him that he has the knowledge necessary to help him solve his problem if he just trusts his own judgment.

Lacking the courage to believe in himself, Harry allows his own fear of frailty to defeat him.

# Passing the Test

**Easy as pie**

*Research shows that if people are really taking an exam and dream of doing so they usually get good marks.*

Dream tests can take many forms: a high-school test, a medical examination, or the performance of a play or song. Exam dreams usually engender feelings of anxiety because the test is unexpected or the dreamers feel unprepared, forget everything that they know, or fear that they are simply not up to the task. Some dreamers have even reported that in their dreams they have studied dutifully for an exam and have walked into it expecting to do reasonably well, only to find that they have been studying the wrong subject. Alternatively, they may find themselves struggling to pass a test that they know they actually passed years ago. Similar dreams involve public speaking, singing, or acting, when the dreamer walks out to deliver a speech or song, only to find that his mind is blank.

## Be prepared

Gayle Delaney explains that at her Dream Center she first asks her students to confirm whether the dream came the night before an actual test. If so, she asks the dreamers whether they felt prepared or unprepared. Although dreamers are often well prepared, they may be such perfectionists that they become overanxious and start to question their abilities. In such cases, Delaney states that this shows that the dreamers need to address issues of self-respect and pedantry.

Next, Delaney asks the dreamers to examine the details of the exam to ascertain whether it represents a test that the dreamers face in waking life and, if so, how they cope with it. If the dream is a recurring one, she asks the dreamers to relate it to deadlines and "tests" faced in the workplace and in domestic life.

If the dreamers state that the test is impossible because it is illegible, on the wrong subject, or blatantly unfair, Delaney asks them to describe the people who set the test, in order to assess what they represent in their waking lives. She maintains that if dreamers decide to tackle a subject that they are not prepared for, they are showing signs of meeting the demands on their time and rising to the challenge of dealing with the unexpected without undue anxiety or self-recrimination. Both William Domhoff and Calvin Hall believe that dreams mirror waking life. This would indicate that people who have exam dreams are facing a test of some kind – emotional or actual.

### More Information

Alfred Adler maintained that these dreams mean that dreamers are not ready to face their problems, and that they should directly relate their feelings in the dreams to conscious issues.

**High-flier**

*Bill has just been promoted to head the financial division of a multinational corporation, over many of his more senior colleagues.*

# THE WRONG QUALIFICATIONS

Bill dreams that he has been promoted to head the financial division at work, the youngest executive to be appointed to this position. Suddenly, rumours start that his college credentials are pure fiction. To his horror, he discovers that this is true: his college reports that he failed a test and his degree is therefore not valid. He cannot understand this, because he knows that he has all the right credentials. His friends begin to desert him, disappointed by his duplicity. He is summarily fired from work. He must go back to college to pass the crucial test that will validate his degree and give him back his job and self-respect.

In Bill's dream, his former friends begin to gossip about his lack of experience and qualifications.

## Dream Analysis

In their book, *The Dream Oracle*, David Melbourne and Keith Hearne devised a fixed, universal set of dream meanings based on the alphabet: A=Avarice, B=Brevity, C=Consequence, etc. Dreamers read the meanings for each letter and, before sleeping, ask for a problem-solving dream. They usually have a dream in which a particular letter features in a major way and wake to recognition of the letter and the meaning of the dream.

On waking from his dream, Bill realized that his dream was peppered with the letter "f" (finance, failed, fired) throughout. He immediately thought of *The Dream Oracle* and the meanings for this letter. The letter "f" referred to Faith. This was a rite of passsage for him: he had been trusted and rewarded by his peers. Instead of questioning his right to gain promotion over some of his colleagues, Bill should believe in himself and his abilities.

In Bill's dream he must go back to college to attain the necessary qualifications. In reality he has them already.

# The Body Beautiful

**Standing tall**
*Upright posture in a dream
suggests good management of your
spiritual and intellectual powers.*

The body, or a part of it, often
features in dreams. Although your
interpretation should reflect your
circumstances at the time, you should
also consider three explanations:
physical, symbolic, and compensatory.

On a physical level, dreaming of a
particular part of your body may be
prodromal, warning you of impending
illness or health problems. If you dream
of choking on food, or a restriction in
your throat, your dream may be
symbolically highlighting the fact that
you are unable to digest or embrace

new experiences and ideas, or that you
have trouble communicating. Finally, the
dream may simply be compensating in
dream life for what the body lacks in
waking life, so if you feel that you are
overweight, your dreaming mind may
make your body slim and svelte.

## Heads and hands

The head is the centre of intellectual,
rather than intuitive, wisdom, so if you
dream of a head, it may be suggesting
that you are over-intellectualizing. If the
head is grotesquely large, perhaps your
unconscious mind is urging you to curb
any egotistical behaviour

Your hands are among the most
expressive parts of your body and
therefore symbolically represent your
expressive side. Betty Bethards suggests
that you pay close attention to which
hand is significant in your dream.
Because the left hand receives energy
and the right hand gives it, if your left
hand is injured in your dream, this
signifies that you are cutting yourself off,
while if the right hand is injured, you

are giving too much of yourself away.
The fingers, too, play a key role in
dreams. If you see a finger pointing in
a specific direction, Bethards maintains
that it is either showing you the way or
targeting a problem. If it is a finger of
blame pointing at another, however, be
cautious, for it is really pointing at
another part of you: you need to accept
responsibility for your actions.

## The back

If the back is significant in your dream,
you should consider the main support
structures in your life, as well as your
strength of character. Standing straight
and tall in your dream may indicate
good management of your spiritual and
intellectual powers, whereas being bent
or weak suggests that you may be
spineless and ineffectual.

### More Information

Eyes are synonymous with enlightenment in
dreams. If you are sightless, have clouded
vision, or your eyes are shut, you are blinding
yourself to the truth and should look inwards.

**Shy and reserved**
*Daniel is a naturally reticent man who is coming to terms with the end of a long relationship.*

# I'M LOSING MY TEETH! Daniel dreams that

he is in the bathroom, having just finished shaving. He looks at himself closely in the mirror to check for razor cuts, and suddenly realizes that something strange is happening to his teeth. He feels some of his teeth crumbling away to powder in his mouth, and, as he opens his mouth to spit out the bits of tooth, others simply fall out of his mouth. He tries to hold them in and to force them back into his gums, but more and more of his teeth fall out and soon he is completely toothless. Daniel looks at himself in the mirror with horror, wondering how he will ever be able to smile or talk properly again.

*Daniel dreams that as he looks in the mirror his teeth start dissolving or falling out.*

## Dream Analysis

Tooth-loss dreams, together with hair-loss dreams, are among the most common dreams, with most of us dreaming them at some stage in our lives. Artemidorus, the Greek author of *Oneirocritica* (see pages 38–9), was one of the first people to identify these dreams. He stated that the upper row of teeth represented householders, while the lower set represented slaves. In his interpretation, dreaming of the loss of either set therefore indicated some form of turbulence in that particular part of the house. The loss of both sets of teeth, on the other hand, suggested that the whole household would suffer in the future.

Some writers have suggested that tooth-loss dreams reflect a waking anxiety about encroaching old age and loss of looks. Daniel found Jeremy Taylor's interpretation to be the most plausible, however. Taylor believes that dreaming of tooth or hair loss points to the dreamer's lack of self-confidence or feelings of impotence. He insists that the very fact of remembering such a dream indicates that the dreamer is well equipped to handle any situation effectively and creatively. Daniel took comfort from this fact because his girlfriend had recently ended their relationship. He has felt inadequate but is now going to put the past behind him.

Daniel's horror at his tooth loss is immediately followed by panic at the thought of appearing in public ever again.

# Embarrassing Dreams

**Invisible nudity**
*In many dreams of nudity, other characters in your dream seem oblivious to your discomfort or lack of clothing.*

Several dreams induce feelings of extreme embarrassment or humiliation. Amongst the most common are dreaming of being naked in a public place, of seeing excrement everywhere, and of needing to go to the lavatory. These dreams often point to your fear of being found wanting in a given situation.

## Naked in public

Despite being naked in public, what is odd about these dreams is that you are generally completely powerless to find a place to hide. You will also probably find that everyone else in your dream is quite indifferent to your appearance and obvious discomfort.

Unlike Freud, Gayle Delaney maintains that if you dream of public nudity, you are merely working through your feelings of vulnerability. For her, your reaction, and that of the strangers in your dream, are highly significant, for they not only reveal the levels of your self-confidence and vulnerability, but indicate that your anxiety about your "exposure" may be unwarranted.

For both Jeremy Taylor and Robert Van de Castle (who worked out a comprehensive coding system for dreams with the psychologist Calvin Hall), clothes represent the persona, or public identity, of the dreamer. Consequently, when you are naked, you have allowed more of your true self to show in waking life than is usual or acceptable. For Jeremy Taylor, if the onlookers ignore you, your self-revelation has gone unnoticed, but if they show outrage, it indicates that damage control is needed because the exposure of your true self has upset the people around you. For Robert Van de Castle, if you are ignored by "the public", it may mean that revealing your true self to those who do not wish to know it is pointless, while if you are ridiculed by those around you, it shows their insincerity, not your shortcomings.

### Excrement everywhere

Jeremy Taylor maintains that dreaming of excrement is one of the most illuminating dreams. He believes it suggests the need to purge feelings, often of shame. He stresses that this dream shows you how bad things really are, and that unless you evaluate all the "excrement" in your life, you cannot hope to move forward and change.

#### More Information

Research has shown that men dream of being naked in public more than women, perhaps because they are less adept at emotional intercourse and feel vulnerable when revealing their innermost feelings.

**The substitute**

*Sam's father died young and Sam has worked during every school holiday to help support his mother and younger sister.*

# I'M DESPERATE TO GO

Sam dreams that he is in a busy town. He needs to go to the lavatory urgently and goes into every shop, hotel, and restaurant that he comes to. He searches everywhere, but there are either no lavatories or they are already occupied. He is aware that if he does not find a free lavatory soon he will have to relieve himself on the street. He finally sees a sign for public conveniences and rushes in, only to find that the room is full of lavatory pans but none of them is in a private cubicle.

In his dream, Sam simply cannot find anywhere to relieve himself and is completely desperate.

Although dreaming of needing to urinate often means that you really do need to go to the lavatory and that your sleeping brain is responding to your physical need, it also symbolizes problematic emotions and thoughts that have not been resolved in waking life. As Jeremy Taylor puts it, in order to stay healthy, you need to empty your bladder at regular intervals: urination and defecation are biological functions, and if you do not do either, the toxins that will thereby build up will poison you. Although you can decide when and where to urinate, ultimately you cannot ignore your need to urinate indefinitely. In the same way, a urination dream highlights your need to explore and express your deepest thoughts and inner emotions, and, if necessary, to purge yourself of feelings that are impure or outmoded.

Sam realizes that he has felt angry at his father's death for some time and has thrown himself into work in order to mask his feelings of guilt and grief. Sam's dream is telling him he must urgently resolve emotions that once sustained him but are now crippling him. The fact that Sam searches for somewhere private is also quite common. After all, everybody needs to find a safe place to let go of extreme emotions.

When Sam finally finds somewhere to go, it is utterly exposed and he finds it impossible.

# Sexual Dreaming

**Vive la différence**
*Not surprisingly, men's and
women's sexual dreams differ
quite radically in content.*

Every one of us has sexual dreams at one time or another. Some of these are highly erotic and sensual while some are more uncomfortable and worrying, such as dreams of changing sex, having a different sexual orientation, making love in a public place, being caught in the act, or of making love to someone other than your partner.

Women's favourite sexual dreams are of men who are experienced and considerate of their emotional and sexual needs and who are turned on by the dreamer. Men's favoured sexual dreams are of women who are completely uninhibited and ready for absolutely anything.

## Freudian slips

Freud was the first really to explore the sexual context of dreams. For him, however, dreams merely showed what he believed to be the true natures of men and women. When analysing the symbols that Freud claimed represented sexual imagery, Calvin Hall found 102 symbols for the penis, 95 for the vagina, and 55 for the sexual act. Freud's insistence on virtually everything in a dream being symbolic of repressed sexual desire has, perhaps, perpetuated the discomfort that most of us feel when discussing an erotic dream.

## A positive approach

Gayle Delaney, in her book *Sensual Dreaming*, has explored this area extensively. As she says, exploring and understanding sexual dreams can give you an insight into sexuality. At a deeper level sexual dreams can help you to understand, and come to terms with, any inhibitions, psychological issues, fetishes, or perversions.

Remember, however, that sexual dreams are not just about sex. According to Delaney, they can be synonymous with emotional problems, or, if they are dreams about being with an unexpected lover – particularly one of a different sexual orientation – may represent a different part of your psyche, qualities that you aspire to, or a particular goal in life.

But what if you are raped in your dream? Delaney and Faraday both suggest that this may be simple thought transference: you may subconsciously feel that you are being cheated by someone, and this suspicion is being brought to the forefront of your mind.

### More Information

A 1996 survey undertaken at the dream laboratory at Hôpital Sacré Coeur in Montreal, Canada, revealed that women had almost as many sexual dreams as men.

**Mister Right**

*Juliette has always been anxious to please her parents, particularly in her choice of boyfriend.*

# WHAT'S GOING ON? Juliette dreams that she

and her new boyfriend, Carl, are at her parents' house, which she is looking after while they are on holiday. She and Carl have a leisurely meal together, then a luxurious bath, and finally go to bed. The foreplay is exquisite and the sex the best she has ever had. Just as they both reach a peak, the door opens and in walk her parents. Juliette and Carl freeze, mortified to be caught making love, especially here. But Juliette's parents talk to them both as if the situation were quite normal, and her mother potters around chatting, tidying up, and dusting. Although Juliette and Carl are paralysed with embarrassment, her parents don't seem to notice anything odd.

*In Juliette's dream, every part of the evening with Carl is wonderful.*

## Dream Analysis

When interpreting sexual dreams, the Jungian analyst and clinical psychologist Dr. August Cwik asks you first to take into account Jung's compensatory function of dreams. Ask yourself what your conscious approach to sexuality is. If the people in your dream are people in your life, an objective interpretation of the dream is appropriate. At this level, your dream may be trying to teach you something about your relationship with others. Since it is unlikely that your parents are intruding in your relationship, their appearance in such compromising dream circumstances probably represents an emotion that you identify with them that affects your sexual relationships.

Juliette's dream suggests that something associated with her parents is affecting her relationship with Carl. She believes this is probably that she has always felt the need to have a boyfriend that they approve of. She concludes that since she is more worried about the presence of her parents in her dream than her parents are about what she and Carl are doing, she should trust her judgment and not be so anxious about their opinions.

Juliette and Carl are appalled to be found in bed by her parents, but they seem completely oblivious to the lovers' predicament.

# How's the Weather with You?

**Weather report**
*The weather in your dreams engenders the same emotions as you experience in waking life.*

Just as you can be affected by changes in the weather in your waking life, so the weather reflects your emotions in dreams. You may lurch from being happy and full of life during the spring and summer to suffering from seasonal affective disorder and feeling depressed during the dark winter months. Remembering that the qualities of light and heat in your dreams are no different from the feelings that they give you when you are awake should help you to interpret weather dreams.

If you are particularly conscious of the weather in your dreams, take careful note, for it is a key symbol. If the weather is peripheral in your dreams, however, do not let it confuse your judgement as to the overall meaning of a dream, for it may merely reflect the fact that you are feeling too hot or cold in bed.

## Bring me sunshine

We all feel better when the sun shines, so if it is shining on you in your dream you can be sure that the message is a positive one. If the sun rises in glorious technicolour, it may signify a vital breakthrough in a relationship or project that you are involved in, or may simply be an affirmation that you are on the right track.

Since clouds obscure the sun they may be portents of impending problems, but if the sun comes out from behind them you may be sensing brighter prospects ahead.

### Rain, rain, rain

In dreams, as in waking life, rain can cast a distinctly gloomy aspect on your situation, but remember that it also washes away the dust and grime. Consider the other circumstances in your dream and decide whether the rain reflects a minor depression or the foiling of all your hopes and plans, or whether it is telling you that you should clear your head to be fully prepared for new stimuli.

### The ice maiden

If ice is a repeated symbol in your dreams, consider whether you have frozen your emotions in some way in order not to be hurt. Are you being insensitive or too sensitive? Have you cut yourself off and put yourself "on hold"? If you find yourself on thin ice while dreaming, you are aware that you are taking a risk that you shouldn't be taking, regarding either a situation or a relationship.

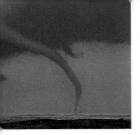

**Hurricane Andrew**
*The elemental power of a hurricane or tornado is terrifying in the dream world, just as in reality.*

# THE HURRICANE
There's a storm coming, and not just any storm: it's a hurricane that is wiping away everything in its path. Whirling in perpetual motion, it has an almost mesmeric power. You watch it approaching from a distance. Sweeping inexorably towards you, you see the thin column of devastation leaving shattered remnants in its path. Funnelling up from the earth, the pillar of wind seems to reach into the heavens throwing out debris and rain. Winds whip around its centre at 160 kilometres an hour. Water vapour, sea spray, and storm detritus are catapulted into the atmosphere. Roof tiles seem to lift off houses effortlessly, and shrubs cartwheel high into the air. Yet on the periphery everything else is left untouched.

The storm may be warning you of an overwhelming surge of emotion that you may find impossible to control.

## Dream Analysis

Many dream interpreters believe that dreaming of stormy weather of any kind implies the arrival of sudden forces which are beyond your control. These may be inner transformations, an emotional deluge, or a surge of passion.

Jeremy Taylor has noticed that such dreams have become increasingly common in recent years and offers a different interpretation, however. Although he points out that dreaming of hurricanes is hardly surprising, since the world's weather is steadily changing as a result of global warming, he does not feel this is sufficient reason to dream of them. He is convinced that there is a collective consciousness at work. It is only with creative awareness, by growing and developing ourselves, that we can take moral responsibility for the planet.

Taylor argues that although we are highly skilled at manipulating our physical world, we are still novices at understanding the deepest levels of our internal world. In other words, we have knowledge, but no self-knowledge. Although he firmly believes that only the dreamer can accurately interpret the dream that she has dreamed, he suggests that hurricanes in dreams symbolize both individual and social change, which we intuitively accept as being necessary and inevitable. These dreams ultimately reflect the dreamer's as yet incomplete or unresolved relationship with deep, fundamental spiritual or psychological issues. When hurricane dreams are remembered, Taylor argues that it is clear evidence that the dreamer is prepared for increased self-knowledge and self-belief.

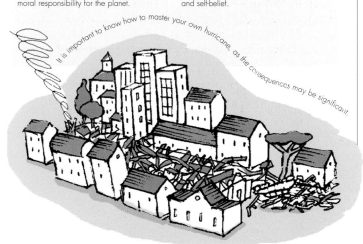

It is important to know how to master your own hurricane, as the consequences may be significant.

# The Dream Landscape

**A new perspective**
*Interpreting the qualities of your
dream landscape will give you insight
into your own inner landscape.*

Ernest Hartmann, Professor of
Psychiatry at Tufts University School
of Medicine in Massachusetts,
proposes that the setting in which your
dream takes place is vital, because it is
a vivid metaphor for your emotional
state. It gives a distinct snapshot of what
the dream is about, in terms of mood,
emotion, and the issue with which the
dream is concerned.

Your dreams play with all of your
actions and emotions, and juxtapose
every thought, feeling, and memory.
But, as Hartmann says, your dream
state is like therapy, in that, unlike your
normal waking hours, it offers a safe
place in which to make emotional or
psychological connections and to
experience and resolve any problems
that may arise.

## The Garden of Eden

If you accept Hartmann's theory, then
lush, green meadows, colourful plants
and soaring, leafy trees all spell out a
positive outlook, emotional well-being,
and a measure of success. If you
glimpse them in the distance from a
barren outcrop, then perhaps you are
feeling stressed and depressed, but can
sense good times ahead. Maybe you
see a vision of rural bliss, but suddenly
notice beer bottles, some rusty cans,
and a refrigerator abandoned in a
hedge. If so, perhaps you are feeling
content, and just a little complacent,
and your dream is telling you to wake
up to reality. If you envisage marshes
or deserts, you are probably on shaky
emotional ground or your relationships
are stagnant and it's time to move on.

The terrain that you see in your dream is also important. Gently rolling hills generally augur well for your path in life, as opposed to craggy mountain peaks, which may imply that you are in for a challenge.

## The tree of life

Trees are universal symbols of growth, with their roots representing foundations, their trunks strength and support, their limbs your capabilities, and their leaves the fruits of your efforts. If your tree is flourishing, with wide-spreading branches, you are emotionally healthy and loving, but you must remember to prune it regularly to eliminate any dead wood and encourage future growth. If your tree is unloved, untended, and bare, then your self-esteem is lacking for you are not honouring your potential.

### More Information

Although the dream setting is important, so is what you do in it. Because your dream and dream imagery are unique to you, only you can accurately interpret them.

**Difficult choices**
*Lucy has a difficult decision to make between career and her friends and family.*

# BRIDGE OVER TROUBLED WATER

Lucy dreams that she is travelling on foot with friends and family. After a while her companions disappear, and she is left facing the rest of the journey alone. She comes to a rope bridge slung over a very deep canyon. Peering over the edge, she can see the rushing water below. She instinctively knows that this is the only way to reach the other side of the canyon, but is afraid to set foot on the bridge. Finally, she closes her eyes, grasps the ropes on either side of her, and steps out. As she does so, the bridge becomes firm beneath her feet.

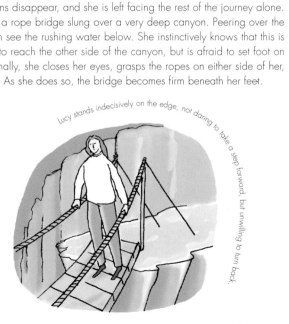

*Lucy stands indecisively on the edge, not daring to take a step forward, but unwilling to turn back.*

As Gayle Delaney reiterates, your dream setting is never coincidental, for it denotes the part of your life that needs addressing. By using Delaney's interview technique and outlining every detail of the dream to a friend, as well as how she felt about it, both in dream time and in waking life, Lucy realized that the bridge represented a transitional period in her life. She had recently been offered a very good job, which represented a significant career advancement, but also entailed her moving to the other side of the country. She had agonized long and hard about whether she wanted to leave her family and friends behind, because she was so happy and settled where she was. Lucy's dream taught her that she was ready for the change and that her family would be with her in spirit wherever she went.

When Lucy finally commits herself to the crossing, she walks safely to the other side where her long-lost companions are waiting for her.

# The Urban Jungle

**Ivory towers**
*Buildings often represent the structure that we try to give to our everyday lives.*

An outdoor dream environment may not necessarily be rural and bucolic: it may be a densely populated, brightly lit city or a dark, forbidding citadel.

Calvin Hall and Robert Van de Castle have created a comprehensive coding arrangement for dream imagery, the dream setting being one of the main categories in this system. In analysing countless dreams, they have concluded that men's dreams tend to take place in a familiar, outdoor setting, while women's dreams are usually set in a familiar, indoor location.

## Happy homes

In dreams, houses represent your internal world. Gayle Delaney suggests that if you dream of someone else's home you need to know all about that person in order to find out why this dream setting is relevant to your current situation. She further advises that if the house is your own childhood home you should think back to when you lived there to ascertain whether the issues that you are now dealing with have their roots in your life at that time. On the other hand, if you dream of your current home, it is perhaps warning you of an impending domestic problem.

## Castles and churches

Larger buildings suggest an enormous amount of energy and potential. Castles are places of safety and defence, so you could construe from dreaming of a castle that you are either secure in your current situation or that you are being unnecessarily defensive and reclusive in your waking life. Churches are outward symbols of spirituality, so if you dream of one, your dream may be alerting you to a need to explore your spiritual path more fully.

## Places of learning and healing

Schools, colleges, universities, and libraries are all institutions that are devoted to learning, so dreaming of any of these places may indicate that you need to locate some specific information, that you have a valuable lesson to learn or that you need to seek the advice of someone who is wiser or more experienced than you are.

Dreaming of hospitals can serve one of two functions: first, to warn you about the state of your health, or that of a friend or family member, and alert you to signs of impending illness, or, second, to encourage you to relax and restore your sense of well-being.

### More Information

If you dreamed about a specific house, it is worth checking to see whether it is in good condition or whether it needs renovation, and, if so, where it needs it.

**Standing still**
*Tom has been longing to start his own business for some time but has lacked the courage to do so.*

# THE HOME MAKER

Tom dreams that he has purchased a dilapidated old mill house that has been derelict for years. He notices the broken glass in the windows and notes that the staircase has several missing treads. A vagrant seems to have camped here recently because there are ashes in the fire grate and a strangely comforting smell of wood smoke. Tom embarks on the renovation work himself. He cleans out the basement, repairs the woodwork and masonry, builds a new staircase, decorates, and moves his furniture in.

*Tom is overjoyed at the prospect of transforming the derelict mill building into a home.*

A building under construction can symbolize all of the projects and ideas that you are working on, or the plans that you are making. In Tom's dream, signs of a recent fire impinged on him quite clearly, and he deduced from this that the fire had cleansed both the house and himself, beginning his own process of transformation. He had been procrastinating about his career and future, having worked as a photographer for a large firm for many years. Although he had been longing to start his own company, he had never had the courage to do it. He interpreted the original state of the derelict house as evidence of his misgivings. He had recently made the decision to go it alone, however, and was feeling fired with new energy and enthusiasm. His vision had become clearer, his work was better, and clients seemed to be flocking to him.

Tom realizes that renovating and decorating his dream house symbolizes his newfound energy and drive.

# A Room with a View

**Home is where the heart is**
*Houses reflect so much of ourselves that
it is hardly surprising that so much action
takes place there in our dreams.*

When Calvin Hall and Robert Van de Castle created their comprehensive dream-coding system, both men and women reported that their most familiar indoor dream setting was their home, followed by their workplace.

## The attic and the basement
Dream researchers all agree that the attic represents your highest aspirations, your goals in life and your spiritual awareness, while the basement symbolizes the darkest corners of your unconscious mind that you do not wish to address: your fears, worries, and phobias, as well as your untapped talent. The other symbols that appear in each of these places, along with the feelings that they engender, are also highly significant. If the attic, in particular, is cluttered, for example, you may need to shake up your ideas; if, on the other hand, it is bare, you should consider changing your life in some way to incorporate some new interests and bring some focus to it.

## Stairs and corridors
Both stairs and corridors are devices that link one room with another. It is always important to ascertain where the stairs or corridor lead in your dream. Walking along a corridor may suggest a pivotal moment in your life, when transformation is about to occur, so which rooms did you go from and to? Likewise, stairs link the lower rooms of a house with the upper rooms, so where did the stairs take you: up or down? These details will give you clues.

## Kitchens and dining rooms

These two rooms are usually at the very heart of family life. The kitchen is a creative room in which you cook, so are you cooking up plans and schemes to present in the dining room, which is synonymous with nurturing and sharing? Are they places of domestic chaos or of cosy contentment? What feelings do you experience in your dream?

## Bedrooms and bathrooms

Beds play a highly significant role in our lives: we retire to them to rest, relax, and refresh ourselves, and also to explore both sexual relationships with lovers and nurturing ones with children. The expression "You made your bed, now lie on it" is very true in the dream world. In a bedroom dream, you are given the opportunity to bridge the gap between your conscious and unconscious mind.

If you dream of a bathroom, however, perhaps it is time to clean up your act or get rid of outmoded ideas (see also pages 114–15).

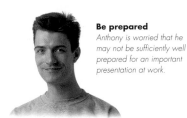

**Be prepared**
*Anthony is worried that he may not be sufficiently well prepared for an important presentation at work.*

# THE LIVING ROOM
Anthony dreams that he is throwing a party for friends and work colleagues. Suddenly he notices that he is dressed as a clown and that the room has changed. All his friends start laughing and pointing at him, and when he looks at everyone he realizes that they are all strangers. He leaves the room and changes quickly into different clothes, wipes the make-up off his face, and then returns. When he walks through the door, the room is exactly as it was at the beginning of his dream, complete with all of his friends, who behave as if nothing had happened.

*Anthony dreams that he is dressed as a clown and his home and friends are unfamiliar.*

## Dream Analysis

The living room is the social room, the room in which you interact with others. In Jungian terms, this room could represent the persona, or public face of the house-owner. Anthony related this dream directly to his workplace. He had gone out on a limb to please new clients, but had not got his figures together in time to present them at his last meeting. He had felt inadequate and open to ridicule, and had vowed not to pursue his project any further. His dream encouraged him to believe that he did have a good idea and that he should pursue it. He realized that he was too worried about what his colleagues would think of him if he presented his idea when he felt a little unprepared, and recognized that his lack of self-confidence was holding him back.

Anthony realizes he is worried about what others will think of him, rather than the quality of his ideas.

# Travelling on Land

**Travelling in style**
*The condition of the vehicle in which you are travelling may well indicate your current quality of life.*

Whenever you travel in your dreams, it is a comment on the course that you are taking in your waking life. The dream may simply be a reflection of a journey that you are about to make, but is usually a symbolic interpretation of your spiritual journey.

Dreams often show you the terrain, which may be hilly or difficult, highlighting problems that you are facing that may be holding you back. And how are you travelling? Are you the driver or the passenger? If you are in the driving seat, then you are in control; if you are the passenger, you may be relying on, or being influenced by, someone else. Are you dreaming of an arrival or a departure? Arrival gives you a sense of how well you have succeeded at what you set out to do. Is the place at which you have arrived familiar? If not, are you confident about exploring it or else filled with dread? Departure suggests a new beginning, so how do you respond to it? With anticipation or with reluctance?

## Trains and buses

As modes of public transport, buses and trains direct your attention to your social behaviour and relationships. Because both forms of transport follow a set route in the company of others, you may want to think about the course that your life is taking and whether you are just being carried along.

You may experience trouble with timetables, miss the train, bus, or a connection, arrive too early or too late, get off too soon or go past your destination. All of these scenarios

suggest that you are having difficulty
in your waking life and need to re-
evaluate things urgently. Ann Faraday
advises you to question what it is within
yourself that doesn't want to grasp the
opportunities that are open to you. She
suggests using the empty-chair
technique to ask yourself what was
on the train or bus, and why you
unconsciously chose to miss it.

## Cars and driving

The car mirrors the dreamer's
personality, how you handle life,
and the way in which you wish to be
perceived by others. What kind of car
you are driving is important. Is it flashy
or understated? Is it clean or rusty? And
what about the driver? If it's you, you're
in control; if not, you are losing control
over the events in your life.

### More Information

Walking, as opposed to using transportation,
suggests that you are capable of managing
that part of your life's journey on your own and
that you are in control.

**Rest and recuperation**
*Colin has been very unwell
recently and has not had
time to recuperate before
starting work again.*

# HEADING NORTH
Colin is in a van, heading north.
It is a Sunday. The driver is his father, at a younger age. They usually travel
westwards, but Colin does not want to ask his father why they are going north
instead. Suddenly the road narrows and is blocked by two long wooden
ladders. Beyond, men are rebuilding walls on either side of a rural road which
twists away into the distance. Somehow Colin knows this is the only way north
and sees little point in turning around to find an alternative route. Moreover,
Colin realizes that his father intends to stay there until the work is complete,
which will not be until Monday morning. In the meantime, they must stay
where they are and wait patiently until the work has been finished.

Although Colin knows that the driver is his father, this man looks more like his father in his mid-30s.

## Dream Analysis

Colin writes out this dream at length because it seems to relate directly to the ME that has laid him low for the previous five months. He interprets the dream as reflecting his physical state and the bodily repairs that are under way. He has already taken wrong turnings by doing too much too soon, and has suffered for it. It is significant that it is a

Sunday, a day of rest. It is also significant that he is the passenger. His "other", a wiser version of himself, is trying to show him what he should have recognized before now: recovery will take time, and he must be patient until the process has been completed.

The van's path is blocked by ladders and men working and there is little prospect of moving on until the following day.

# Water, Water Everywhere

**Ducks to water**
*Watery dreams convey your emotional
state in waking life, so can you keep
your head above the water?*

Gayle Delaney suggests that
water has no single meaning
in a dream: it can have a
multitude of significances, depending
on how it is seen or felt and what body
of water it constitutes. However, water
is usually taken as symbolizing the
emotional body. Whether clean or
muddy, deep or shallow, choppy or
still, it shows your emotional state at the
time of the dream. So if you dream of a
drought, what might you be missing in
your emotional or spiritual life? If there's
a flood, are you in danger of becoming

overwhelmed by the strength of your
emotions? If the water's freezing, are
you being cold and undemonstrative?

## Baptism

Many dreams of water feature
cleansing or washing. In baptism, water
washes away the sins of the world. If
you dream of washing or bathing, is it
possible that you are trying to cleanse
yourself spiritually, in order to enter a
new phase in your waking life? Or,
more prosaically, are you perhaps
behaving like Lady Macbeth, trying to
rid yourself of negative emotions or to
shed something of which you are
particularly ashamed?

## Oceans, lakes, and streams

The sea can be regarded as
representing life itself, or the nature of
cosmic consciousness. The depth of the
sea is important in your dream.
Depending on the circumstances, a
shallow sea could imply a certain
superficiality, while a deep sea could
indicate either that you have deep

emotions that are waiting to be tapped or that you are out of your depth. Waves represent the ups and downs of our emotional lives and mirror our inner agitation or peace accordingly. So if you're riding a wave on a surfboard, you may be mastering powerful emotions, while if you are sitting on the shore watching the waves, you could be recharging your batteries.

Lakes tend to reflect your emotional responses, and may indicate that you should look at your shadow side in order to resolve a problem. Rivers, like roads, show the course of your life, so if you dream of a river, it's important to note whether the water is clear or murky and, if you are in it, whether you are swimming upstream, against the current, or whether, like a fish, you feel at home in this environment.

### More Information

Boats symbolize the body – particularly the emotional body – so it's important to know whether you're at the helm and in control, or adrift or sinking in a stormy swell.

**The bottom line**

*Chris is overworked, overstressed, and beginning to question his capacity to cope.*

# DROWNING

Chris is a publisher with a wife and two preschool-aged children. He dreams that he's in a pool, swimming lengths underwater, when he suddenly notices other swimmers, their faces hidden behind goggles, overtaking him. They stare at him as they push ahead. The swimmers are all around him, hemming him in, and Chris can't rise to take in air. His lungs bursting, he opens his mouth and the water gushes in. He feels himself sinking to the bottom of the pool. He's drowning, but is powerless to prevent it happening.

Chris, at first happy swimming underwater, begins to feel threatened by the faceless swimmers above him.

## Dream Analysis

Dreams of drowning are frightening, and occur so commonly – among swimmers and non-swimmers alike – that a profound folk memory appears to be at work here. Older interpretations of such dreams suggest loss of life or property in the waking world, but we now see them as a form of symbolic drowning. Since water often symbolizes anything emotional or feminine in dreams, is Chris feeling that he is emotionally drowning in a situation or relationship? He is putting in very long hours at the office and taking work home in the evenings. He's "drowning" because he feels overwhelmed by work. He

is also afraid that he isn't up to the task and that he's being left behind. His sense of inadequacy is clear from the fact that anonymous swimmers keep overtaking him. When he feels himself drowning, he cannot think or act rationally, so he does not fight his way to the surface. Yet his dream is also trying to tell him that he has the ability to do so. He was not out of his depth initially, but was swimming happily underwater until he suddenly noticed how well everyone else was doing. It was at that point that his self-confidence was shaken and his anxiety took hold.

Chris's lack of confidence overtakes rational thought and practicality. He allows himself to sink.

# Flying Dreams

**Free as a bird**
*Flying dreams are usually pleasant, filled with an unparalleled sense of freedom and joy.*

What do the dream experts say about flying dreams? Freud made a strong association between dreams of flying and sexuality, the effects of sexual desire, orgasm, the phallus, the womb, and the foetus within it. He argued that flying dreams in men could be interpreted as symbols of the erect penis, and that flying dreams in women could indicate the unconscious wish for one. It is certainly fair to say that the exhilaration experienced in a flying dream can be compared to sexual ecstasy. More recently, dream researchers have taken the approach that flying dreams are synonymous with a sense of personal achievement, and that the overwhelming feelings in such dreams are the positive ones of confidence, certainty, success, and self-possession. Most researchers believe that the meaning of the dream is not literal but psychological, and that you should pay attention to the details in your dreams in order to fathom the messages that are inherent in them. Gayle Delaney places particular importance on this factor, maintaining that you should ask yourself why you had the dream at that particular time, what issue in your life led up to it and whether you anticipate its resolution.

## How high can you go?

Does the height at which you are flying have any significance? What if you are flying too high and burn your wings, like Icarus? If so, perhaps your unconscious mind is telling you that you have been over-ambitious. Alternatively, perhaps you are hovering high in the clouds, which suggests that you may have been over-idealistic. Maybe you can glimpse the ground from your lofty height, which suggests that although you have high ideals, you still have your feet on the ground. Similarly, you may dream of a kite, which flies high in the sky, but is still anchored to the ground. This dream indicates that although your ambitions are elevated, you are not an idealist and still retain the practicality and grounding in reality that are necessary to achieve your goals.

You may also lose altitude and plummet so close to the ground that you are in danger of crashing into it. Betty Bethards argues that this shows you fear breaking out of your self-imposed inhibitions in order to enter a higher dimension and seek true enlightenment.

### More Information

Betty Bethards maintains that, because of the nature of flying dreams, if we ask any question at all in such a dream, the answer will arrive.

**Altitude**
*How high do you fly?*
*It is important not to be*
*over-ambitious, or, like*
*Icarus, your wings may*
*be singed.*

# FEARLESS FLIGHT

You are flying high in a clear, azure sky, your arms outstretched like wings. You are lifted by each thermal, drifting and turning on the breeze. The view of the earth below is beautiful: you can see everything in vivid colour and detail, as if you are observing the world in miniature. You feel exhilarated and powerful. Tucking your arms close to your sides, you throw your head forward and embark on a swallow dive. You feel the wind rushing past your cheeks and ears, flattening the hair on your head. At the last minute you pull back and skim across the tops of the trees, revelling in your skill and the freedom that you are feeling.

Flying dreams may simply be an indication that you are releasing yourself from self-imposed limitations.

## Dream Analysis

We love to dream of flying: it gives us a sense of limitlessness and a wonderful feeling of euphoria. We feel capable of anything, fully in control of our destinies and yet totally free. We can transcend the time–space continuum just by willing it to occur. Flying dreams are more common in children and older people, perhaps because children want to soar higher than they are actually capable of doing, while older people yearn to escape the constraints of limited movement.

Betty Bethards and Anthony Shafton, the latter a dream analyst and author of *Dream*

*Reader: Contemporary Approaches to the Understanding of Dreams*, both maintain that flying dreams may mean that you have consciously left your body and are able to transcend different dimensions. But Shafton states that flying dreams indicate a number of other messages, too: a simple wish to rise above a present difficulty, for example, or the warning of an impending illness; of feeling high, feeling low, or of paranormal phenomena, including out-of-body experiences and astral projection. In fact, Shafton suggests 24 possible interpretations.

*Flying dreams give you a unique perspective on both yourself and your current situation.*

# Falling Dreams

**Jumping without a parachute**
*Sometimes your dream is telling
you to bail out of a situation before
you go down with the plane.*

Falling dreams can be linked to
flying ones: first exhilaration is
experienced, then sudden shock.
Interestingly, more women report having
falling dreams than men. Freud made a
connection between this type of dream
and sexuality, the notion of sexual
indulgence – or of the "fallen woman" –
for him being synonymous with the
implicit symbolic message conveyed by
the dream. Yet Freud also conceded
that the falling dream could be a replay
of the childhood trauma of falling out
of bed, or an expression of fear.

Today's dream researchers are
more likely to widen Freud's sexual
interpretation to include anxiety about a
particular sexual relationship or concern
about sexual mores, but they also
suggest that the meaning is perhaps
closer to "falling from grace", or even
"pride coming before a fall". Lori Reid
suggests that falling dreams could be
motivated by feelings of self-disgust if
they are linked to a moral dilemma,
such as committing a shameful act,
breaking a promise, betraying
someone, or even losing face. Both she
and Gayle Delaney maintain that you
should look closely at what precipitates
the fall itself. Could it be that this dream
is not so much driven by feelings of loss
of status or respect as a fear of failure
or lack of confidence?

## Early warnings

There is a superstition that if you hit the
ground during a falling dream you will
die. Although this is not the case, Reid
hypothesizes that, while it is rare, a
falling dream may certainly warn of

impending danger. She surmises that your eye may have taken in some aspect of your life that could be potentially hazardous, and that by making you dream of it in the context of a falling dream, your unconscious mind is bringing the danger to your attention in this shocking manner to make you act on your observation.

Betty Bethards and Robert Van de Castle both suggest that dreaming of falling may imply a loss of control over a given situation or that you may simply wish to "bail out" of a problem. Your dream has identified the need to be centred and grounded. If the fall is an exhilarating experience, executed with grace and ease, Bethards contends that you are centring yourself on, and grounding yourself in, your body and thereby experiencing the full "you".

## More Information

Dream analysts who have researched universal dream themes, of which falling is one, claim that more than 80 per cent of us have dreamed of falling at least once.

**A fall from grace**

*Peter has recently felt out of depth at work and unable to complete his projects.*

# A FALL FROM A CLIFF

Peter dreams that he is standing on the edge of a sheer cliff, looking down at the sea. He feels uncomfortable and at odds with nature. He takes off his shoes and socks so that he can feel the earth and grass beneath his feet. He experiences an uncontrollable urge to leap off the cliff and fly. Spreading his arms, he pushes off hard with his feet. He intends to glide but finds himself falling down the cliff face. Peter wakes up to find himself lying half in, half out of his bed.

Many of us, like Peter, experience an overwhelming urge to fly in our dreams, but find ourselves falling instead.

There is a common phenomenon that is linked to falling dreams and associated with the descent into sleep: you are tucked up in bed, feeling warm and relaxed and just dropping off to sleep, when you begin to feel that you are falling; reaching out to stop yourself, you return to full consciousness with a jolt. This is known as a myoclonic jerk, or spasm. It occurs because your muscles relax as you are falling asleep, until you ultimately reach a state akin to paralysis, but just as you are losing strength and muscle tone, your brain sends a message that revitalizes your muscles. Once you have woken up and have realized what happened, you will sink into

an even deeper sleep. Dream analysts also believe that a drop in your blood pressure or body temperature may account for a falling dream, since both of these conditions may provide the sinking sensation that your unconscious mind could translate into a falling dream.

At first Peter believed that this dream was simply his unconscious mind warning him that he was about to land on the bedroom floor in a heap. When the dream remained firmly in his mind, however, he began to revise his opinion, finally realizing that he was feeling out of his depth at work and was beginning to question his own judgment and ability.

Dreaming of falling headfirst is extremely frightening. Peter, like most of us, wakes suddenly and with a real feeling of terror.

# Climbing

**Snakes and ladders**
*Where are you on the ladder of life? Rocketing upwards or plummeting down?*

Dreams about climbing are fairly common, particularly among ambitious people. They seem to relate directly to your sense of self-esteem regarding material worth, career success, and social standing. They can also allude to your progress towards spiritual enlightenment, however, particularly if a mountain is involved (see pages 124–25).

## Climb every mountain

Most dream analysts believe that the mountain symbolizes the course of your life, with the pinnacle representing a source of wisdom and knowledge. Scaling the summit is therefore akin to finding the ultimate in spiritual enlightenment rather than success in more worldly affairs.

But how was the climb in your dream? Was it rocky, precipitous, and dangerous? Did you struggle to climb it, or did you find that you reached the top as if you had wings on your heels? The ease with which you climb the mountain corresponds to the ease with which you move towards self-knowledge in life. If you dream that you are sitting on the summit and surveying the world below you, you have surely achieved what you set out to do. But what if you were not climbing upwards, but going downhill? If you dream that you are climbing down the mountain, it suggests you are taking a wrong path in some aspect of your life.

## Stairs and ladders

Both stairs and ladders signify much the same as climbing a mountain, albeit in a more systematic way: step by step, you are climbing the ladder of your life or career. Watch out for missing rungs though, which represent obstacles, as well as for the quality of the treads, which could be either rickety or solid. The more sweeping and grand the staircase, the more grandiose your ambitions. Conversely, if the stairs are shabby, damaged, or very steep, your ascent will be much more problematic. If you are going up the stairs, you are on the right path, but if you are going down them, you are slipping down the ladder of opportunity. If you are running up and down the stairs, you are feeling confused, indecisive, and muddled. Lori Reid makes one further observation, noting that if you are going downstairs to the basement you are not failing, but acknowledging that you are ready to face your deepest fears.

## More Information

Freud's interpretation of dreaming of a mountain ascent was quite different, for he drew a parallel between climbing up a mountain and sexual climax.

**No head for heights**

*Isabelle has a morbid fear of heights and is trapped in a lift that does not seem to function properly.*

# THE GLASS LIFT
Isabelle dreams that she is in a glass lift on the third floor of a building. She presses the button for the top floor. The doors close but the lift does not move. She tries again. This time the lift moves but stops on the fourth floor. The doors do not open. Isabelle is inexplicably terrified that she will end up in the basement. She becomes aware of a bird hovering near the lift. She opens her eyes fully and looks around her. The view is breathtaking. Feeling an overwhelming sense of calm, she presses the button for the top floor and the lift rises smoothly.

In her dream Isabelle dares not open her eyes to look around her for fear that she will have a panic attack.

## Dream Analysis

Since escalators and lifts ascend to the highest, and descend to the lowest, places in a building, they convey a similar message to stairs, but with one telling difference: the ascent or descent requires minimum personal effort. For Isabelle, the lift's responses to her instructions are nightmarish until she acknowledges the irrational basis of her fear. Her terror of going down to the basement is linked to her inability to open her eyes. She does not want to visit the basement because there she will have to confront her sense of inadequacy. The bird that enters her consciousness symbolizes her freedom to choose: either to be scared that she will be found wanting or to move forwards fearlessly. Pressing the button, she finds that her progress is smooth and effortless.

The sight of a bird flying outside the lift gives Isabelle the inspiration she needs to regain her composure.

# Animals

**Snakes alive**
*Jung believed that we are born
with a fear of snakes and this certainly
is a common and universal instinct.*

Rosemary Ellen Guiley, author of
*Dreamwork for the Soul*, believes
that animal dreams reveal more
about your psychological, emotional,
and physical states than any other
dream because they draw on the
primitive parts of your mind. If you
understand the key characteristics of the
dream animal and how you interact
with it, you will be able to interpret the
message of the dream, which is usually
that you are neglecting a particular
emotional aspect of yourself in your
relationships with others.

## Snakes

With the exception of Freud, who
interpreted the snake as a phallic
symbol, most dream interpreters feel that
the snake dream represents the
awakening of spiritual energy and
growth. Jung stated that the snake is an
archetype for transformation, change,
and perhaps God, although he said
that it could have negative attributes.

Betty Bethards maintains that if the
snake bites you in a particular area you
should look at the dream closely, for it
will tell you which part of your energy
you are blocking. If it bites you in the
throat, for example, this indicates that
you are having trouble communicating
with others or expressing yourself.

## Dogs

We usually associate dogs with loyalty
and friendship, so the appearance of a
dog in your dream may suggest that
you need to look closely at a certain
relationship to ascertain what is wrong
or right with it. Because dogs also
represent our masculine side, if the dog

is aggressive, you may need to channel
any frustrations that you are feeling into
more positive outlets.

## Cats

Interpreters once saw the appearance
of a cat in a dream as a harbinger of
misfortune. Today, however, analysts
believe that the cat represents the
feminine side of our nature. Because the
cat is an independent creature, it may
symbolize your need to be free to
explore your femininity, particularly if the
cat in your dream is a wild cat. If the
cat that you dream of is domesticated, it
may indicate that you are concerned
about "civilization" and about society's
expectations of you.

## Horses

The horse is a complex symbol.
Dreaming of a stallion can indicate
power and potent sexuality; a beast of
burden can symbolize exploitation;
while dreaming of galloping on
horseback can signify freedom and
unity with nature.

**Catty remarks**
*Amy's best friend at school seems to have deserted her and is making unkind observations about her.*

# THE CAT

Amy's family have a dog and two female cats and she has grown up with all of them. She dreams that her favourite pet, Marmalade, a gentle, affectionate ginger cat that comes to her and sits on her knee the minute she gets home from school, suddenly turns on her, spitting and hissing. She is horrified because she has always regarded this particular cat as her own. Amy thinks that perhaps she may have startled the cat, so she tries to calm her down. As she reaches out to pick her up and stroke her, Marmalade lashes out with her claws and scratches Amy's right hand.

*Marmalade, Amy's favourite cat, always welcomes her when she comes home from school.*

## Dream Analysis

Animal dreams are common, particularly in children, who dream about animals more consistently and more often than adults. The Swiss researcher Inge Strauch, who has examined this trend closely, has shown that although boys tend to dream about wild animals and girls more about pets, both usually make the animal the central character in their dreams. In adult dreams, by contrast, the animal often represents a threat against which the dreamer retaliates. This is perhaps unsurprising, given that we constantly bestow human characteristics on animals and vice versa. We know exactly what is meant by such sayings as "He's a pig!", "She's a cat!" or "What a rat!", associating the more negative traits of the person thus described with what we perceive as being

the negative characteristics of that particular animal. (But it is interesting to note that Westerners think of the rat, for example, as a betrayer and coward, while the Chinese respect it as an astute and resourceful creature.) If the association that you make between the animal that you are dreaming of and a particular characteristic is very strong, it will not be difficult for you to draw a conclusion about what is wrong in your life or with a particular relationship.

When Amy was asked whether anything in her life reminded her of the cat in her dream, she reported that she had recently found out that a girl whom she had previously regarded as one of her best friends had been saying nasty things about her behind her back. The parallels between friend and cat are clear.

Marmalade, like her friend, seems to have found something about Amy that she dislikes.

# On the Wing

**Swan or ugly duckling?**
*It is important to take note of the
bird you see in your dream and
what it represents to you.*

Birds appear in many guises in
dreams. Although the kind of bird
that you dream about is significant
in symbolic terms, of equal importance
is whether you see a single bird or a
flock of birds. In addition, it is important
to note whether the birds are flying free
or are caged, as well as whether you
feel reassured or menaced by them in
your dream. If you can identify and
recognize what the bird's behaviour
signifies to you, it will also tell you a
great deal about yourself and your
current situation in life.

## Birds of a feather

The majestic eagle, the king of the
birds, is the symbol of ultimate power,
since it indicates your ability to accept
responsibility for your actions and take
care of your needs. If you see an eagle
in a negative light in your dream,
however, it may suggest that you are
searching for "prey" and are being
overbearing and threatening in your
behaviour in waking life.

The duck, on the other hand,
suggests an innate ability to cope with
any emotional situation that is thrown at
you. Although a duck's natural
environment is water (see pages
140–43), because it can fly and walk
as well as swimming and diving, it
demonstrates great flexibility. Like the
duck, the swan glides across the waters
of emotion, yet is also able to soar to
great heights. If you dream of a swan,
ask yourself what it suggests to you. If it
is beauty, purity, and tranquillity, these
are the qualities that it symbolizes to
you. Dreaming of a black swan may
suggest the mystique of the unknown.

The dove is a universal symbol of peace, so seeing this bird in your dream is likely to bring you a great sense of tranquillity, harmony, and spiritual awakening.

## Bees and butterflies

Do you associate bees with a hive of industry? Do you see them as natural providers, or do you associate them with a nasty sting? Whichever association your conscious mind makes is the right one for you. Similarly, because you may regard butterflies as being flighty and superficial, these may be the symbolic meanings of a butterfly in your dream. Yet butterflies can also be seen as symbols of transformation, or as accurate and startling affirmations of rebirth into a newer, brighter, and more illuminating existence.

### More Information

Birds are normally associated with spiritual freedom and the ability to soar to new heights of awareness without being held back by any material ties.

**Responsibility**
*Stephen is unwilling to face the fact that he must take responsibility for his own company and workforce.*

# THE OSTRICH

Stephen dreams that he is in a vast plain that is dotted with a few windswept bushes. One of the bushes suddenly moves and stands up. As it begins scratching around in the dirt and then buries its head in the sandy ground, he sees that it is an ostrich. It remains motionless, its enormous wings folded over its back and head. An owl and a vulture suddenly appear out of nowhere, flying in from Stephen's right. The two birds swoop down and settle side by side on the back of the ostrich.

Like the ostrich, Stephen has been sticking his head in the sand, unable to make necessary changes.

## Dream Analysis

Rosemary Ellen Guiley stresses the importance of the number three in dreams, for she believes that this number represents the higher self, or intuition, urgently trying to break through to the waking consciousness. She advises you to pay close attention when dream events or symbols occur in threes.

Stephen woke from this dream with a sense of fresh clarity. He had been struggling with a new business venture which was going horribly wrong. He had not been able to meet the demands of his suppliers and distributors and did not know how he would pay his staff. For him, the ostrich represented the fact that he had buried his head in the sand, pretending that all would be well in the end. He knew that he had to face up to his responsibilities, but had felt unable to admit that he was in over his head. The appearance of the owl and vulture was highly significant: the vulture suggested that he had to clean up his act and abandon his outmoded beliefs and practices in order to see clearly the path ahead, symbolized by the owl. Feeling revitalized and refocused, Stephen saw how he could make sweeping changes that would ultimately boost the performance and profitability of his company.

For Stephen, the three birds all represent different aspects of himself.

# Mythical Creatures

**Howling at the moon**

*The she-wolf can be a positive or negative image. She can be a carer of orphaned young or she can be vicious.*

It is in dreams of monsters and mythical beings that Jung's archetypal figures really come into play. It seems that we all dream of these creatures, and that they vary only according to cultural stereotype or historical context. These images can often be some of the most significant in the dream world and figures like the devil and the angel, the wolf and the lamb symbolize aspects of our personality. In order to complete, or individuate, the whole personality, we must meet the needs of each of these sub-personalities. Dreams give us the chance to do so.

## Werewolves

Werewolves are symbols of fear, anger, and violence. They represent both Jung's shadow archetype and highly antisocial behaviour in the form of your deepest, most aggressive, animal instincts, which you either cannot face or find hard to acknowledge. You may not see them as solid forms, but as shadowy figures that bring a sickening sense of foreboding.

## Vampires

Like werewolves, vampires are linked to the forces of darkness, but with one additional characteristic: they are parasites. If you dream of vampires, you need to search within yourself to ascertain what part of you "lives off" others. Perhaps you are relying too heavily on another person for support, or you are living your life through their talents. Alternatively, it may be that someone else is sucking the energy out of you. You need to recognize whether you are the perpetrator or the victim, and therefore in what area of your life changes need to be made.

## Angels and godlike animals

In the Judaeo–Christian tradition, angels are messengers from God. It is therefore not difficult to draw a parallel in the dream world: dream angels are messengers from your higher self that have an important lesson to convey. They are diametrically opposed to demons and devils, who call upon your darkest nature, tempting you to deny responsibility for your actions and to pass the buck.

You may also dream about animals that have godlike wisdom and capabilities. These animals are also vital components of your psyche, for they represent the wisdom of innocence, the instinctual, simple knowledge that is often suppressed by the business of living.

### More Information

The dragon is a universal symbol of wisdom and strength, whose fire dispels illusion and negativity. Slaying a dragon suggests that you have conquered your fears and gained new self-awareness

**Compromise**

*Cathy is plagued by self-doubt and is always the first to back down in an argument.*

# DEMONS IN MY HEAD

Cathy dreams that she is at the centre of a ring of demonic red figures, who are screaming abuse at her. Surrounded by these vile creatures, she puts her head into her hands, willing them to go away. Finally, goaded beyond all reason, she lifts her head and screams "What do you want with me? Why are you torturing me? Why do you want to hurt me?" The figures then change and appear to emit a golden light. As one, they say to her, "What makes you think that we want to hurt you? We are here to help you. You have nothing to fear from us. Why are you so afraid?" On looking into their eyes, she sees love and understanding. She holds out her hands and the figures seem to dissolve as she touches them.

Cathy dreams of a ring of demons who torment her beyond endurance.

## Dream Analysis

Frederick van Eeden, a gifted lucid dreamer, coined the term "lucid dream" in an article that he published in 1913 in the *Proceedings of the Society for Psychical Research*. In "A Study of Dreams", he reported having had a dream in which he was surrounded by demons. The demons changed their appearance on a whim and harassed him constantly. Finally, after an altercation with them, he began to recognize each one, and, having done so, woke up feeling refreshed and serene. In his article, he made the point that facing and fighting the demons that had tormented him had caused his terror of them to disappear.

In Cathy's case, her dream conveyed the message that she was able to face even the most unpleasant situations with equanimity. As a result, she became much more adept at dealing with crises in her personal life, as well as in the workplace. She learned to stand her ground and to express herself, whereas previously she would have backed away and avoided confrontation.

When Cathy has the courage to face her demons, they become her guardian angels.

# Food and Drink

**Fruitful**
*Dreams convey internal responses to external stimuli. Dreaming of food is closely associated with the inner self.*

Most dream analysts would argue that food and drink are symbolic representations of spiritual, intellectual, or emotional nourishment. If we cook food for others, or it is cooked for us, there is usually a loving intention behind the act of cooking that conveys an instinct to nurture or be nurtured. But equally, in the language of dreams, you might be "cooking up" a new scheme or "cooking" the books, "stewing" over a problem, "brewing" an inspiration, or may be "hungry" for a specific goal, perhaps power, knowledge, or love.

The circumstances in which your meal takes place, as well as the quality of it, are highly significant. Cooking for yourself indicates loneliness and a search for emotional fulfilment, while cooking for others (particularly if the meal is lavish) indicates a total expression of love. If the meal is skimpy perhaps you unconsciously realize you are being mean with your affections. And if you have trouble cooking it for any reason, could you be trying too hard or too little?

And what of the dream food itself? What does that signify? Fruit, which frequently appears in dreams, is often seen as an expression of sexual energy or promise, but – like eggs – can also represent fertility. Tucking greedily into a lush peach may imply your lust or longing for a sensual experience, for example, or may alternatively symbolize your own "fruition" in some way. Puddings are always regarded as comfort food by dream analysts, so dreaming of them may express your yearning or need for support and reassurance from others.

### Bread and water

Dreaming of bread and water is
common. Lori Reid suggests that your
mind may associate the bread in your
dream with financial concerns, whereas
dream analyst and astrologer Julia Parker
suggests that bread relates to character
development and urges you to scrutinize
the dream closely, examining every fine
detail to assess your spiritual progress.
Betty Bethards, on the other hand,
associates bread with communion
bread, the bread of fellowship and the
awareness of your place in God's
universe. She suggests that dreaming of
bread could signify your need to grow
in spiritual awareness. In a Christian
context, if the bread is linked to water
or wine, it reinforces the spiritual
message, as water represents purification
and wine the blood of Christ.

#### More Information

If your dream meal tastes bitter or unpleasant,
it almost certainly indicates self-disgust or may
highlight a specific problem or a relationship
that is unpalatable to you.

**Faithful friends**
*Alice has come through a very traumatic divorce with the help of her closest friends.*

# THE FEAST

Alice dreams that she has cooked a meal for her closest friends. She has taken the trouble to find out what each person's favourite food is and has cooked a dish for each of them. She finds herself comparing herself to the central character in *Babette's Feast*, a film that she loves, because she is delighting in taking infinite care to get everything right: the food, the wine, the silver cutlery and crystal glasses, flowers, and lighting. Her friends arrive and they have a wonderful evening, full of laughter.

Alice dreams of cooking all her closest and dearest friends the best meal they have ever tasted.

## Dream Analysis

Food and drink often appear in dreams. There could well be a simple physiological explanation for this: you may be hungry or thirsty and your unconscious mind is compensating for the fact. Since food and drink figure prominently in your waking life, it is natural that they should feature in your dream world, too. Yet food and drink in dreams should be viewed as more than just nourishment. The way in which the meal is prepared and served, as well as the circumstances in which it is eaten, should all be taken into account. In addition, what you are eating is important: is it bitter or sweet, delicious or tasteless? All of these factors may indicate whether the food, or what it represents, is nourishing the mind, body, or spirit.

One of the first questions that Lori Reid asks a dreamer is "What were your feelings when you awoke?" Alice reported feeling very special. She cannot remember ever having felt so loved or appreciated. She revealed that she had gone through a particularly traumatic and lonely time after her divorce, but that her friends had been wonderfully supportive. With their help and her own determination, she soon found a new purpose in life.

The meal is a huge success because of the wonderful sense of camaraderie that the friends share.

# Peopling Your Dreams

**Mirror images**
*Like Alice in* Through the Looking Glass,
*the images in a dream may be
distorted in some way.*

Using the analogy of Lewis Carroll's book *Through the Looking Glass*, Anne Faraday describes dream elements as like being seen through a looking glass. This is because although some are direct mirrors of the waking world, others are distorted and utterly strange and unique to the dreamer.

## Close relations

People probably play a leading role in most of your dreams. Faraday contends that if they are intimately related or connected to you – lovers, children, parents, close friends, and colleagues, for example – then they are direct representations of themselves. The critical issue in your dream interpretation is to ask what they were doing, what was happening to them, and to assess the overall setting and action of your dream. She suggests that the prime question that you should be asking yourself is what your dream is trying to convey to you about your current relationships with these people.

Sometimes, however, family members, friends, and colleagues represent part of your personality, often a skeleton in the closet that you have not quite exorcized.

## Passing strangers

If an unknown figure plays a leading part in your dream, Faraday insists that you should first try to work out if they symbolize a particular organization, event, person, or place, or, if not, whether they represent some aspect of yourself. You will probably be able to make a correlation if you connect your dream stranger with someone you know, but linking them with an element of your own personality can often prove more complex. It may be that they symbolize some dichotomy in your psyche; some issue that has not been resolved. If your stranger is a child, it may indicate that you are struggling with a traumatic childhood memory that has remained in your unconscious mind.

## The glitterati

Like Delaney, Faraday suggests that you use the technique of association to see if public figures in your dreams correlate either to the characteristics of people you know in waking life or to your current situation. Could they be showing you what you need to succeed, or to overcome a particular problem?

### More Information

According to Fritz Perls, every element of your dream represents an aspect of your personality. Although they are linked to form the whole character, each acts independently.

**Unloved**
*Claire feels that her family neither respect nor value her fully.*

# MY FAMOUS LOVER

Claire dreams that she is romantically involved with a famous movie star. This actor is synonymous with heroic roles involving great bravery, skill, and strength, but also charm, wit, and imagination. Although he appears as he is in real life, all of his screen qualities seem to be intact. In the flesh, he is everything that his screen persona is cracked up to be. Claire can see that every woman around them is incredibly jealous of her because her star has eyes for no one else.

*Claire dreams that she is having an affair with a famous actor who is besotted by her.*

Gayle Delaney emphasizes that it is important to ask yourself whether the star in your dream appears as they are in real life or whether they appear as their most famous screen incarnation. She also asks you to describe what they are like, what they are doing in your dream, and why you like them. Do they remind you of yourself or of anyone else in your life? Do they share any of their characteristics with you or anyone else you know? You may often dream of a particular star because you aspire to the characteristics associated with them, or sense that you may be developing some of their skills or abilities.

Delaney suggests that if there is nothing about the star that strikes a chord with you, you may be feeling the need to boost your self-esteem.

Claire had felt for a long time that she was being taken for granted by her husband and children. She perceived that her contribution to family life was undervalued and longed for some recognition. In her dream she felt special, needed, desired, and cherished.

Claire's famous lover is besotted with her, despite every other woman vying for his attention.

# Colour Symbolism

**Colour blind**
*Do not place too high a degree of
trust in conventional meanings for colours
– the dream experience is uniquely yours.*

It is generally understood that colours
form part of the collective unconscious
and therefore that a particular
association made by any ethnic group,
ancient or modern, should be
considered relevant and important.

## From red to yellow

Red is primarily associated with
passion: love and anger, lust and
gentleness, tenderness and strength. But
it is also a universal symbol for "stop".
Red corresponds with the base chakra,
and Betty Bethards suggests that its

appearance may indicate your need for
energy. The Chinese regard red as a
joyful colour, and it is the colour most
frequently worn by Chinese brides.

Yellow is a happy colour that
represents the sun, the light of life and
general well-being. Yellow corresponds
to the third chakra and works to relieve
fear and cowardice. If the yellow is of
a muddy or dark hue, you should take
care, however, for treachery or
faithlessness may be at work.

Orange represents love and peace,
energy, and harmony. If you dream of
the fruit, you may need nurturing.

## From green to purple

Green is the colour of nature and new
growth. It is a therapeutic colour and
works on the heart chakra to restore
balance, heal pain, and bring hope.
However it can also represent being
"green", in the sense of being naïve,
as well as being "green with envy".

The blue-to-purple colour spectrum
indicates different levels of emerging
spirituality and truth. Azure blue is

connected with aspiration and life ambition, while a mid-blue shade is relaxing and has the effect of focusing the mind. A dark blue tone is much more sombre and contemplative and indigo hints at spirituality and divine protection. All shades of purple indicate wisdom and emerging knowledge.

## Black and white

White represents purity, simplicity, innocence, and new beginnings, while black is the colour of sadness, loss, and death. When black predominates in a dream, it signifies a trauma that has been buried deep in the unconscious mind. White corresponds to the crown chakra, which represents enlightenment. A speck of white in a mainly black dream represents a beacon of light.

### More Information

Chakras are whirling vortices of energy within the human body, each with a specific action. For instance, the throat chakra relates to communication skills. Chakras are known by their numbers rather than their position, for example: the second chakra.

**Jilted**

*Anna has been jilted by her boyfriend and is left feeling angry and jealous that he is in a new relationship.*

# BEING GREEN WITH ENVY

Anna dreams that she sees her old boyfriend, Paul, at a party. Paul, who left her for another woman, has a new girl, Stephanie on his arm, whom both Anna and Paul knew years ago. Both of them are dressed in red and are completely absorbed in each other. When Anna looks down, she realizes to her horror that she is wearing exactly the same dress as Paul's new girlfriend, although hers is green.

Anna dreams that she sees her ex-boyfriend with his new girlfriend, an old acquaintance.

Research suggests that although you usually dream in colour, you only remember it if the colour is particularly significant. Colours in dreams are often vivid, and women tend to see more colour than men. Betty Bethards links colours to the chakras, stating that colours have different properties and vibrations and symbolize different levels of awareness. She suggests that colour dreams often indicate where your energy is blocked or lacking, and therefore which chakra is out of balance. If the colour is implicit in an object – a ruby, an orange, or the sky, for example – your unconscious mind is focusing on the symbolism of the associated colour and not on that of the object itself.

Anna analysed her dream and found that she associated Paul and his new girlfriend, Stephanie, with passion and love because the most significant thing that she remembered about the couple was the colour of their clothes. To her discomfort, she also realized that the most vivid thing that she recalled about herself was her dress: not only was she wearing the same dress as Stephanie, but it was green, suggesting to Anna that she was yearning for something that she could not have and was "green with envy". She therefore resolved to let go of her feelings for Paul and to move on.

Anna is horrified to find that she is wearing the same dress as her rival but hers is green, the colour of envy.

# Numbers and Numerology

**Paint by numbers**

*Numbers in your dream can illuminate a particular problem or strike a chord within you when you come to interpret the dream.*

Numerology – the study of numbers and their significance – is based on the belief that each number has its own distinct energy or vibration, which is attuned to the rhythm of the universe.

When numbers appear in your dreams, it may be either because they hold some special significance for you or because your mind is trying to tell you something that you have not consciously recognized. Because your dreams work on so many different levels, it is important to remember that they may not only be repeating factual information, but that a symbolic inference can also be drawn. A number will sometimes flash into your head, but more usually you will take note of a certain number of chairs in a room, or lights in a street, and then wonder why this information is so important to you.

## One, two, and three

Number one symbolizes the leader, the pioneer, or simply you, setting out to achieve all of your goals. It is the number of power and authority.

Number two represents duality and balance. Your dream could be telling you any number of things about the relationship that you currently have with your partner, or about an objective that you have set yourself.

Number three signifies the trinity of mind, body, and spirit. It is the number of creativity and intuition and prompts you to be guided by your imagination and inspiration.

## Four to ten

If the number four is stressed, your unconscious mind is urging you to lay a solid foundation for all that you do.

The number five represents the five senses and encourages you to free yourself to follow your dream.

The number six is associated with the family, integrity, truth, and stability.

The number seven is the number of mysticism and inner awareness.

Dreaming of the number eight is considered lucky, for it hints of wealth earned through hard work.

All that is humanitarian is associated with the number nine, which may point to an expanded awareness.

Finally, the number ten represents completion, maybe of a project or aim.

### More Information

Zero is considered to be a sign of the unconscious or the absolute. Because it is a cipher that holds both everything and nothing within it, it symbolizes potential.

# TAKING IT FURTHER

Ann Faraday believes that dream analysis should not be conducted by therapists, but by dreamers, to enable them to develop self-knowledge. As she says, we all have untapped resources that we do not use because we are too busy playing psychological games or indulging in harmful relationships. If you harness the power of your dreams, you can begin to rid yourself of unhealthy emotions or relationships by consciously acknowledging them. There are a number of practical aids to peaceful sleep, many of which are included in this section. You will also learn about techniques to develop lucid dreaming and the hypnogogic state, and to deal with nightmares and recurring dreams.

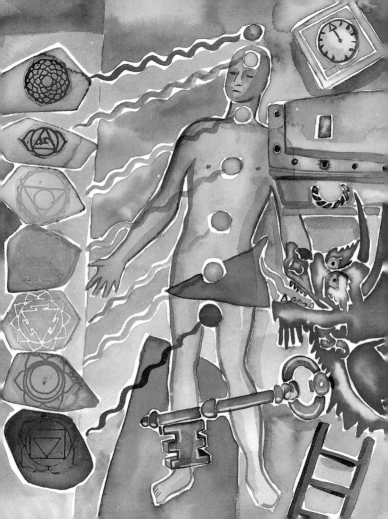

# Herbs and Oils

**Lavender blue**
*Lavender is one of the best-known
sleep-inducing herbs, and is
particularly good for children.*

There is a great deal of folklore associated with herbs and sleep. In the past, lettuce or a mixture of hops and mistletoe were considered highly soporific, and camomile teas or tisanes were used as sedatives.

The classic herbal remedy for disturbed sleep is valerian, particularly when used with passionflower. Valerian was used during both World Wars to help people suffering from shell shock and recurring nightmares, while passionflower is used in Ayurvedic medicine as a cure for sleep disorders.

The French use lime flowers to aid sleep and cure tension headaches. Perhaps the most popular herb for encouraging sleep and preventing nightmares is lavender, which is better known for its sweet perfume, but is widely cultivated for its medicinal properties. The flowers can be used either in the form of a herbal pillow or distilled and used as an essential oil. As well as being antiseptic and antibacterial, Lavender is known to calm and soothe the nerves, relax the muscles and, ultimately, induce restful sleep.

Try out different herbs and herbal combinations to see which works best for you. You could then fill a pillow with your favourite sleep-inducing herbs or make a muslin sachet to drop into your bathwater before going to bed.

## Essential oils

Today, aromatherapy is used as an incredibly effective de-stresser, as well as to balance psychological or physiological problems. Essential oils are extracted from flowers, herbs, trees, spices, and vegetables, from either the flower, leaf, bark, fruit, wood, resin, or bud, usually by means of steam distillation. Some essential oils, like ginger and black pepper, are very stimulating and should be used sparingly, while others, like rose, neroli, and sandalwood, work on the senses; still others, such as lavender and camomile, induce a sense of calmness.

Essential oils can be used to promote sleep in several different ways. One is by sprinkling a few drops of a particular essential oil, or a combination of oils, into your bath before bedtime. The renowned aromatherapist Julia Lawless recommends a combination of camomile, lavender, and rose for a particularly relaxing evening bath. Alternatively, you could place some essential oil in a vaporizer or sprinkle a few drops on your pillow or handkerchief to encourage sleep. Lastly, if you want a sensual massage prior to love-making and sleep, Lawless suggests a mixture of jasmine, ylang ylang, and sandalwood.

# CRYSTALS

The balancing and healing powers of crystals have been recognized for thousands of years. Each crystal radiates a special kind of energy, which works with your own energy system to restore any imbalance. Remember to choose your crystal with care. Crystals somehow attune themselves to your needs, and you will probably find that you will instinctively choose the one that you are most attracted to, even if you had intended to choose a different stone at first.

**Agate**

*is a very effective de-stressing stone.*

**Amethyst**

*is calming, relaxing, and good for promoting sleep.*

**Blue lace agate**

*brings emotional security.*

**Emerald**

*encourages nurturing, defuses muddled thoughts, and aids untroubled sleep.*

**Jasper**

*is a powerful healer that works on all of the chakras.*

**Lapis lazuli**

*opens the heart and encourages trust.*

**Quartz**

*has a sedative effect and promotes inner peace and tranquillity.*

**Rose quartz**

*calms the heart and provides unconditional love.*

**Topaz**

*is a relaxing and rebalancing stone especially effective in warding off nightmares.*

**Adventurine**
*stimulates intuition.*

**Black onyx**
*reveals repressed emotions.*

**Carnelian**
*promotes feelings of self-worth.*

**Malachite**
*protects.*

**Mother of pearl**
*balances and reduces negativity.*

**Rhondite**
*increases self-respect.*

### Cleansing

You should cleanse your stone as soon as you have chosen it by washing it under running water and then leaving it in the open air for a day to enable it to absorb natural light. In the evening, take your stone to your bedroom, and, holding it firmly in your hand, visualize its energy and particular properties permeating the entire room. Now place it next to your bed, or under your pillow, and it will release its healing energy throughout the night.

**Sodalite**
*helps to counter communication problems.*

**Tiger's eye**
*protects.*

**Turquoise**
*balances.*

# A Different Kind of Sleep

**Half-sleep**
*The hypnogogic imagery of a semi-dreaming state is uniquely vivid and graphic.*

You may find that, just as you are falling asleep, you experience a semi-dreaming state. This is known as hypnogogia. It begins before you drift into the first cycle of sleep, when you have not yet gone through all of the physiological changes that sleep induces.

Hypnogogic sleep tends to involve a series of disconnected images or snatches of information, which, although fleeting, possess a vivid, almost surreal, beauty. It often features archetypal figures and bursts of pure colour that are usually symbolic and visionary. If you are lucky enough to experience hypnogogic sleep, you may find that a vision of piercing clarity gives you an acute insight into your current situation.

## Hypnopompia

You may experience similar bursts of incongruous images as during hypnogogic sleep when you are in the state between sleeping and waking. This is known as hypnopompia. Research has shown that the two states are, in fact, so alike that they could both be classified as hypnogogic. Perhaps the only clear difference between them is that the hypnopompic images may more readily endure after waking as a creative solution to a particular problem.

## Hypnogogic imagery

One of the most intriguing, and yet frustrating, things about hypnogogia is its incongruous and hallucinatory quality. Unlike conventional dreams, in which there usually appears to be a narrative thread, hypnogogic images seem to follow each other like vignettes, with apparently no logical association. You may see a mountain at sunrise, for example, followed by a woman sitting reading, followed by a fish swimming in dappled water, followed by a flight of steps or a child wearing a hat. None of the images relates to another, nor do any of them relate to anything or anywhere that you remember.

You may find that the images are sometimes preceded or followed by snatches of conversation that are also completely unrelated and have nothing to do with you specifically. You may even have the sensation of floating, falling, or flying, and your body may give a sudden jerk in response to one of these phenomena.

## More Information

The images and sounds that you see and hear during hypnogogic sleep are very similar to those that you may experience during a period of meditation.

# INDUCING HYPNOGOGIC SLEEP

Enthusiastic dreamers often ask how to induce the hypnogogic state. David Fontana is highly illuminating on this. He suggests that when most of us go to bed we mull over the events of the day until we start to relax and allow ourselves to go to sleep. The key to inducing hypnogogia is to prevent the process of sleep from starting by observing the process as it develops.

**Choosing a chakra**

Fontana advises you to settle yourself as for sleep, and then, without thinking of anything in particular, to retain a form of relaxed consciousness. Fontana himself focuses his attention behind his closed eyes, while others fix theirs on their "third eye", the heart, or the crown of the head. Fontana suggests that the visions that you receive will depend on which place you choose to focus on: if you choose the crown chakra, for example, your visions will probably be transformational; if you choose the base chakra, they may be sensual. Choose the place that feels right for you. Having ensured that your eye muscles are relaxed, look into the darkness. The image that will appear will do so without any conscious effort. It may be so faint and transient that you almost miss it, but it cannot be mistaken for an image that you have willed to appear.

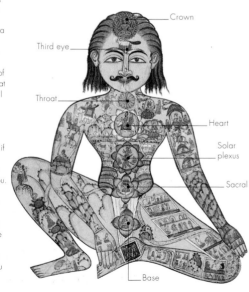

Crown

Third eye

Throat

Heart

Solar plexus

Sacral

Base

## Practice

Fontana stresses that you should not be discouraged if you cannot achieve hypnogogia easily: it may take four or five attempts or even hundreds. He also emphasizes the importance of letting the images come and go. If you strive too hard to capture an image, you will lose it altogether. What is more, you are likely to wake up, and will then find that trying to recapture hypnogogia, or even sleep, is extremely difficult.

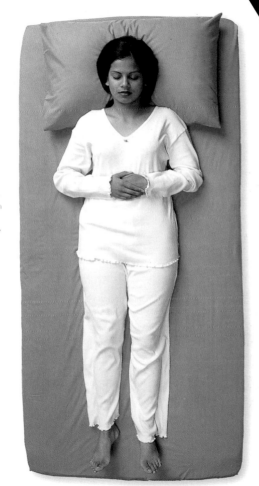

# What is Meditation?

**Focus**
*You can choose to focus on any object that you have to hand; a candle, a pebble, or a leaf.*

Meditation has traditionally been, and still remains, a tool for spiritual growth, but recent research has shown it to be valuable in both combating stress and promoting healing, whether that healing is emotional, physiological (it lowers the blood pressure and slows the pulse rate), or psychological (it assists you to develop intuition and encourages transformation).

## Spiritual schooling

There are numerous meditational schools and techniques, all of which have value, but the truth is that there is only one correct way in which to meditate: the way that is right for you. Many of the most common methods involve breathing exercises (known in yoga as *pranayama*); the repetition of a sound, word, phrase, or mantra; the contemplation of a particular colour, object, symbol, or idea; and visualization. Practising meditation is easy, and even the most sceptical or hesitant of people will find that it helps them to relax and improves their

Many meditators who have experienced hypnogogic sleep attest to the fact that the visual imagery and auditory phenomena engendered are similar to those experienced during meditation.

Many people either confuse meditation with a religious discipline or New Age practices or feel that it is too complicated and time-consuming for them to learn. Yet the best definition of meditation is that it is a means of focusing your attention in order to alter your state of consciousness.

concentration, thus giving them greater access to their unconscious minds and, ultimately, to enlightenment.

When learning to meditate, some of the most important things to remember are what not to do. Don't feel that you have to sit or lie in a particular way. Don't try to force yourself to make something happen. Don't panic if thoughts come into your head – just acknowledge them and let them go: meditation does not entail emptying your mind, simply quietening it down and allowing awareness to enter it. Don't think that you have to "see" something interesting: you may not necessarily see anything, but may sense it instead. Finally, never over-analyse your meditation when you have finished. It is a tool for transformation and reconstruction, not deconstruction.

### More Information

The most common misconceptions about meditation are that it is difficult to learn and requires tremendous discipline. In reality, it is both simple to grasp and hugely enjoyable.

**Gautama Buddha**

*This meditation is one that is said to have been taught by Gautama Buddha. Its aim is to achieve clarity and balance through a calm inner awareness.*

# MEDITATION PRACTICE

When learning meditation it is important not to be too ambitious. Start with 5 minutes a day and gradually extend your meditation period by 5 minutes each time, until you are meditating for 20–30 minutes or more. It is best to sit on the floor or in a chair with the spine straight. Choose as quiet a time and place as possible. It is a good idea to inform those around you of your intention to meditate at a certain time so they will not disturb you. Try the following meditations and see how they work for you:

**Technique**

**1** *Sit comfortably, with your spine held straight and eyes closed. Think about your breathing: the gentle rise and fall of your abdomen and the temperature of your breath as you breathe out through your nostrils. If thoughts, emotions or physical sensations intrude, acknowledge them, but do not follow them. If you realize that your attention has strayed, focus your attention on your breathing. When you have finished your meditation, keep your mind still and tranquil.*

**2** *There has been a huge amount of research on the therapeutic value of colour and its balancing, cleansing, and healing effect. Sit comfortably, with your eyes closed and back held straight. Visualize a luminous ball of light hovering just above your head. Imagine that the light is descending slowly through the crown of your head and filling every inch of your being, sustaining, purifying, and healing as it goes.*

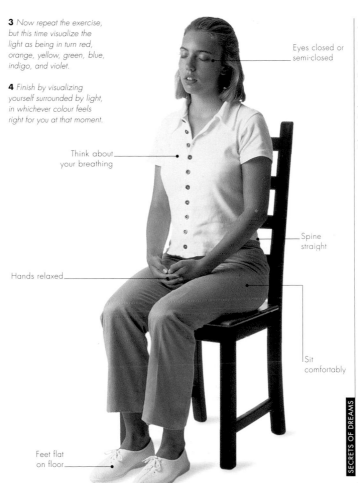

**3** Now repeat the exercise, but this time visualize the light as being in turn red, orange, yellow, green, blue, indigo, and violet.

**4** Finish by visualizing yourself surrounded by light, in whichever colour feels right for you at that moment.

Eyes closed or semi-closed

Think about your breathing

Hands relaxed

Spine straight

Sit comfortably

Feet flat on floor

# Nightmares and Parasomnia

**Eyes wide open**
*Sleepwalkers are easy to mistake for insomniacs who have got up to stretch their legs.*

Research shows that most nightmares take place during REM sleep, and that they are often triggered by an unexpected sound or a feeling of acute discomfort. Although they are very common during childhood and adolescence, nightmares seldom persist into adult life. If they do, they are likely to be recurring dreams: these indicate that some deep-seated problem that has not yet been resolved is troubling the unconscious mind.

Most dream researchers would contend that a nightmare is one of the most valuable teaching dreams that you could have. Betty Bethards maintains that a nightmare either confronts you with a fear that you have magnified disproportionately or with a feeling that you have suppressed, to your detriment.

## Victim or villain?

Nightmares take two diametrically opposed forms: either something terrible happens to you, or you do something dreadful to someone else. The most frequent dream in which you are the victim is one in which you are being chased or attacked (see pages 100–101). The most disturbing nightmare in which you are the villain is the dream of killing someone or standing by and watching while someone is tortured, maimed, or killed. These dreams reveal that there is a part of you that has been repressed, but that urgently needs expressing.

## Parasomnia

Sleepwalking and night terrors both manifest themselves during non-REM sleep. Sleepwalkers often emerge from this type of sleep without having had any REM sleep at all.

People who suffer from night terrors rarely recall anything that happened during them, just an overwhelming sense of dread and horror. The condition is far more common in children than in adults. You will know when your children have night terrors, because they will probably be sitting up in bed, staring maniacally at nothing, and sweating profusely. If you try to embrace them, they will fight to free themselves from your grasp.

Night terrors are distinguishable from nightmares, because after a nightmare, which normally occurs during REM sleep, dreamers will be aware of their surroundings on waking. When children have had night terrors, they will be only partially aware of their surroundings.

**Traffic lights**
*Nightmares are urgent messages from the unconscious to wake up and pay attention.*

# COPING WITH NIGHTMARES

A pounding heart and an overwhelming sense of fear or dread are common to most nightmares. Gayle Delaney insists that although nightmares are disturbing and you would rather forget them, doing so would cause you to miss the message that the dream is trying to convey to you in the most stark and brutal way. Nightmares are like red traffic lights: they are trying to show you a key personal problem or emotional conflict that you should resolve. They often signal that you have ignored or repressed an emotion or a desire to achieve something that is vital to your well-being. Once you have recognized the message, the fear will leave you, as will the nightmare.

**Role reversal**
Jill Gregory, director of California's Novato Center for Dreams, teaches children to confront their nightmares by encouraging them to act them out. She asks them to create a costume for their dream monster and then to act out and narrate their nightmare. Similarly, Ann Sayre Wiseman, a member of the Association for the Study of Dreams, asks children to draw first their monster and then their solution. Although they often begin by killing their monsters, they gradually begin to develop more complex strategies with which to cage or tame them. Illustrating their fear gives the children a safe space in which to confront it and to explore alternatives to running away.

## The dreamcatcher

*Originally made by Native Americans, dreamcatchers consist of a web of threads surrounded by a ring hung with beads, feathers, pebbles, leaves, or shells. According to Native American lore, good dreams filter through the centre of the web and are either dreamed or stored in the adornments to be dreamed another time. Bad dreams, however, are caught in the web and melt away as the sun rises.*

## Dressing up

*By making a dream monster costume and acting out their fear, children learn how to prevent their own nightmares.*

# Lucid Dreaming

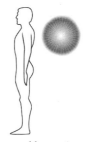

**The assemblage point**

*At this point on the body, pure energy is transformed into sensory perception.*

"Lucid dreaming" is the term coined by the Dutch psychiatrist Frederick van Eeden to describe a dream during which you are aware that you are dreaming and can influence the dream's evolution and conclusion.

## Virtual reality

Lucid dreams have a unique quality of freedom that comes at the moment when you realize that you are actually dreaming. When you become aware of this, the dream seems to unfold at will. Although the framework of the dream is supplied by the unconscious mind, and is unchangeable, the decision on how you will act is your conscious mind's. Peter Fenwick, a neuropsychiatrist at the John Radcliffe Infirmary in Oxford, claims that this is the closest you will come to experiencing virtual reality. It is as if you are conscious while sleeping, and are therefore able to apply your logic and reason to problems and act upon your conclusions.

## Magical passes

According to author Carlos Castaneda, shamans who lived in Mexico thousands of years ago could perceive the universe's energy, and could see each other as spheres of energy.

When a human being is understood as an energy field, the point of greatest intensity is observed at shoulder height on the back, about an arm's length away from the body. The shamans concluded that this spot, which they called the "assemblage point", was the place where the influx of pure energy was transformed into sensory perception and also where it was interpreted. They then discovered that this assemblage point altered subtly during sleep, and that the greater the mutation, the stranger the dream. They intentionally set out to displace the assemblage point while dreaming, in order to experience different fields of energy, different sensory materials and consequently different worlds. The shamans called this technique the "art of dreaming", and found that it gave them an unparalleled sense of well-being. They then refined the technique by moving their bodies in a specific way to permit them to enter this heightened state of acuity during their waking moments. They called these movements "magical passes", and the conscious state of acute perception, "dreaming-awake".

## More Information

In 1867 the Marquis Hervey de Saint-Denys recorded hearing a clock strike in his dream. Aware that he was dreaming, he calculated how much sleeping time he had left.

# INDICING LUCID DREAMING

Not everyone is lucky enough to have lucid dreams, but those who are say that it is an inspiring experience, and that attempts should be made to learn how to do it. Peter Fenwick has done a great deal of research in this area. He maintains that it is much easier to dream lucidly if you have a propensity to do so, but that you will be able to achieve the occasional lucid dream with practice. Stephen LaBerge, of the Stanford University Sleep Center, has certainly trained both himself and his students to become expert lucid dreamers.

**Wake-up call**
There are a number of techniques to induce lucid dreaming. David Fontana suggests that if you are successful with one particular technique, but it later fails, you could try an alternative method. Fenwick maintains that if you wake yourself up after three or four hours of sleep, stay awake until your normal waking time and then go to sleep, you are more likely to have a lucid dream.

## Siesta

Alternatively, Fenwick suggests that if you sleep during the afternoon (when you are generally more alert), you will probably sleep lightly and are therefore more likely to experience lucid dreams. A less intrusive method is simply to ask yourself throughout the day whether you are awake or asleep, and then, while going to sleep, to inform yourself that in your next dream you will be aware that you are dreaming.

## False awakening

Some lucid dreamers report an experience similar to lucid dreaming that is known as "false awakening". Instead of becoming aware that you are dreaming during such dreams, you dream that you are awake, or, perhaps more accurately, you awake to another dream. False awakenings can sometimes seem so real that the dreamer gets up, gets dressed, eats breakfast, and goes off to work.

# Out-of-body Experiences

**Body and soul**
*The theory of the subtle body is fairly common throughout both Western and Eastern culture.*

Out-of-body experiences (OBEs) are surprisingly common. Reports vary from one in 10 to one in 20 people experiencing something of this kind. During an out-of-body experience, you feel as though your consciousness has become divorced from your body, and are able to observe the world without using your physical body or senses.

People who have experienced an OBE commonly report having been embodied in some different way, into a form that can change shape, direction, and location at will. They also often describe a rushing noise and inward vibration, as well as the feeling that their consciousness has become separated from their physical body.

## Body doubles

Throughout history, various theories have been proposed to account for OBEs. Many ancient Greeks believed that we have a second body to which our souls retreat. Plato held that what we see in waking life is but a poor echo of what the soul would encompass if it was freed from the physical body. Both the Tibetan and Egyptian Books of the Dead describe a spiritual energy that can be separated from the physical body and projected elsewhere. The Tibetan Book of the Dead also talks of the *Bardo* body, which is understood to be an exact replica of the human body from which it is separated at the precise moment of death. Indeed, the theory of the subtle body is fairly common within both Western and Eastern cultures.

## OBE or NDE?

Edgar Cayce discussed the possibility of the conscious mind leaving the body and travelling in time and space to explore other worlds. If you have ever experienced an OBE, it is hard to refute the fact that your consciousness is separate from your body, and that it will survive, even if your body will not.

Death appears to be the ultimate OBE. This conclusion presents itself even more forcefully to anyone who has undergone a near-death experience (NDE). Numerous patients testify to the fact that, following a cardiac arrest, they felt as though they were looking down on their bodies, experiencing a sense of lightness and intense vitality at the same moment as the doctor was declaring them clinically dead.

### More Information

Members of the Theosophical Society, founded by Madame Blavatksy in 1875, claimed to be able to undergo out-of-body experiences at will. They called this phenomenon "astral projection".

**Intuitive aid**
*Suffering from chronic back pain was a sign that I was about to have an OBE.*

# CLEAR VISION
There is evidence to suggest that people who experience OBEs can project themselves to those that need them. It is also possible that your first OBE may follow a seminal life experience. This is true in my case: shortly after the birth of my daughter, I had the first of several OBEs. I found that an image of a friend in distress floated into my mind and felt my consciousness detach itself and inhabit her space. I once found myself giving a headache-stricken friend a head massage. On talking to her the following day, she reported going to bed with a migraine and dreaming that I was giving her an Indian head massage, whereupon her headache disappeared. On another occasion, I was suffering from chronic back pain when I knew that I was about to have an OBE. I remember observing my body from above with great clarity, noting what was wrong with it. I knew instinctively how to correct the problem and gave my body chiropractic therapy (which I have not studied).

**Seminal experience**
*Often, the first incidence of an OBE is spontaneous – the result of a seminal life experience.*

## Astral projection

*If you want to induce an OBE, the most common method is a form of progressive relaxation, as follows:*

**1** *Practise deep, rhythmic breathing as you relax every part of your body, concentrating hard on visualizing your body, both inside and out.*

**2** *Concentrate on your breathing while visualizing a glowing sphere of light above your head.*

**3** *Project the number three on to the sphere of light. Do this three times.*

**4** *Visualize the number two three times.*

**5** *Finally, visualize the number one three times.*

**6** *By now you should be feeling no physical sensation as your consciousness moves away from your physical body.*

# Mutual Dreaming

**Dream aid**
*Two or more dreamers participating in one dream can actively set out to solve a particular problem by sharing the same experiences.*

The mutual dream, or *rêve à deux*, as the French call it, is a phenomenon in which two or more people experience a dream together. Although mutual dreaming can be a spontaneous process, it is often planned in advance and incubated with the intention of the dreamers appreciating the same dream. Although normal dreams dreamed by a single individual employ a landscape that is the subjective creation of the dreamer, mutual dreams occur in a shared location.

## The meeting place

Mutual dreams can take place in a number of different ways, one of which is like a rendezvous, in which two or more dreamers meet in the same landscape and appear and act as in waking life. Alternatively, and more commonly, two or more dreamers share the same dream, but walk in each other's shoes. They are not aware of the presence of any other dreamer, but when they compare notes afterwards, they find that they have shared the same experiences, emotions, ideas, images, and events. The distinction between the two kinds of dream is that in one you share a dream landscape, recognize your partner(s) and interact, while in the other you share the dream itself, but are not aware that anyone else is sharing it with you at the time.

## Reciprocal and shared dreams

In a reciprocal dream, a dreamer responds to a dream her dream partner has imparted to her. By picking up on either specific symbols or the entire dream content and action, the reciprocal dreamer dreams a new dream on the foundation of the first. Like Chinese whispers, the dream transmutes as the partners relay their experiences to each other, so that it becomes an interactive dream or series of dreams. In a shared dream, you set out with the intention of encountering another person while you are dreaming.

## Dream helping

Robert Van de Castle sees dreams as the source of an enormous creative power that could be used to influence the course of humanity. In his book *Our Dreaming Mind*, he makes a cogent argument for dreams to be the proper subject of scientific analysis and vigorously defends his work on telepathic dream research. Of particular interest is his account of "dream-helping" rituals, in which a group of dreamers with telepathic powers focuses on a particular person's problem and then collectively dreams to try to solve it.

I am at the seaside, wandering along amongst the debris that a recent storm has thrown up on to the beach. The sun is sinking. I start to collect small, green, pebble-like objects that I find amongst the driftwood and seaweed. I feel compelled to put one of them in my mouth.

**Personal exchanges**

*If you are sharing your dream with a partner, be sure that you feel utterly comfortable with him knowing your intimate secrets.*

# INCUBATING MUTUAL DREAMS

In your normal dream state, you may find that your memory or unconscious mind prompts you to envisage someone who has influenced you during your waking hours. It may be that your interest has been piqued, your sexuality aroused, or your anger provoked. Whether the influence was negative or positive, your dreaming mind may compensate for your lack of action while you were awake to give you the opportunity to resolve the situation. The other person may have been similarly affected by your interaction during the day, and may be dreaming about you at the same time. The mutual dream builds on this, allowing two protagonists to dream together rather than separately.

## Dream Partners

Any dream partnership is a sensitive affair, and you must choose to work with an individual or people whom you can trust. Compatibility and integrity are essential, as Gayle Delaney makes clear in her book *All About Dreams*. Because personal and uncomfortable issues may arise, it can be a mistake to work with someone who is too close to you, for you do not want the dream material to be used against you.

## Partnership

**1** In order to incubate a mutual dream, it is vital that you meet your dream partner(s) to decide on a dream setting that you would like to experience jointly. Review every aspect of the dreamscape that you are working with, taking any insights and feelings that may arise into account.

**2** Before going to sleep, think about your intention to incubate the dream scenario and envisage an image of the other protagonist(s). Phrase a sentence that encapsulates both your intent and the desired dream setting. The sentence needs to be clear, concise, and focused. Once you are happy with it, repeat it to yourself several times and place your trust in the mutual dream occurring.

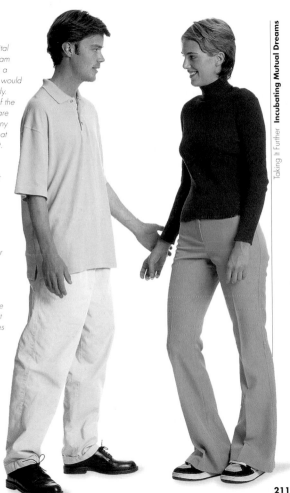

# Recurring Dreams

**Fateful dreams**
*Jung believed that recurring dreams in childhood could presage the future.*

Recurring dreams, which often come in the form of nightmares, are usually giving you an urgent message to resolve an underlying emotional dilemma. They shed light on fundamental issues that you are ignoring while awake. You will often realize what the dream is trying to tell you, but may be reluctant to address the difficulty, causing the dream to recur.

Recurring dreams usually occur for one of two reasons. They either draw an objective, though graphic, portrait of some behavioural pattern that you follow that impacts upon your waking life or they replay a past trauma that has not been successfully resolved. These dreams can actually show you those threads in your life that are preventing it from becoming a balanced whole. You should examine the dream narrative and imagery closely to see what associations you make. What would, or could, you change so that your dream message is understood rather than ignored? Understanding the issue will put an end to the recurring dream, while ignorance will force it to persist.

## Dreaming to reveal the future

Some recurring dreams are prophetic, and Jung believed that recurring dreams in childhood may preview the dreamer's future in some way. Rather than warning you of a past trauma, recurring dreams alert you to, or prepare you for, a certain future. These dreams are often upsetting and disturbing, but this is more likely to be the result of their repetition than any intrinsically fearful quality.

One dreamer reports having repeatedly dreamed of a sunless sky, grey lake, reeds, and pine trees. Native American cooking pots – some broken – and empty canoes are bobbing on the lake. The water is quite rough. The dreamer tells how, aged 27, she went to Canada to meet her biological father, whom she had not seen since she was 4 years old. He insisted that they went to a lake that he knew. They arrived at twilight, but he was adamant that they should get into a canoe and paddle out to the middle of the lake. She suddenly realized that it was the lake from her dreams. She felt compelled to tell him that she knew this lake, that she had dreamed about it all of her life, and that she now knew that she would no longer do so. Indeed, she never had the dream again.

### More Information

In a recurring dream, your subconscious mind is urging you to address a specific problem and will continue to do so until you either respond positively or outgrow the problem.

**Genetic inheritance**
*Do children inherit dreams as part of their genetic inheritance?*

# SECOND GENERATION DREAMS

There is evidence of dreams that are passed from generation to generation. The significance of these dreams is that the original dreamers never told their children about their nightmares until their children had exactly the same dream. None of these dreams can therefore be ascribed to a child visiting a dreamscape that is familiar to them, as their dreams often reflect a movie they have watched. In the case of these second generation dreamers, they are reliving and re-experiencing their parents' emotions, fears, and phobias.

### The ideal home

One dreamer, Lorraine, shares her name and birthday with her mother. Although they look alike physically, they are very different emotionally. Lorraine has had her dream about 50 times over 25 years, and so has her mother. The dream is about moving from a house that she really loves to somewhere that she does not want to move to. Both of them relate experiencing overwhelming feelings of grief at leaving their beloved house for a new one. Although the style of the house is not consistent, the emotion felt is always the same.

## The tower

Another dreamer, Victoria, had the same recurring dream until she was 20, when it stopped. It was a dream of pirates sailing around the top of a tall, grey tower firing cannonballs at her and her family on the ground. The atmosphere was dark, smoke-filled, and terrifying. To Victoria's astonishment, her eldest daughter, Emma, reported having exactly the same dream. Emma even described the tower in Victoria's dream, which Victoria had identified as a water tower near her childhood home, but which her daughter had never seen.

### Dream Analysis

Is it possible that these inherited dreams are a form of shared, or mutual, dream that may happen spontaneously? Can they be transferred in some inexplicable, psychic way, or are they throwing up a past life experience that both mother and daughter have shared? Could these dreams be genetic? Could it be that a foetus not only receives essential nutrients through the umbilical cord, but also its mother's memories and emotions? Since the daughter may inherit some of her mother's characteristics, perhaps she, in turn, has the same sort of fears and therefore the same type of dream. The really interesting thing is that it's *exactly* the same dream.

# Dreams and Quantum Physics

**Split universe travel**
*Theoretically, no contact can be made between split universes but you do not need to make contact because you already exist in each one.*

What is a dream? Is it a world that exists only in your mind? Is it a world that is more real than the physical one you inhabit? Do you catch fleeting glimpses of the next world in it? Does it represent a halfway house between this world and the next? There are no firm answers to these questions, but what if you look at dreams from the perspective of physics, as some quantum physicists have done?

**Many universes**

In 1957, Hugh Everett proposed the theory that numerous parallel worlds exist, and that they continue to be created in bewildering numbers. Many of them are virtually identical to our world, while some are different.

According to the theory, each time a quantum event occurs, the universe splits. With each split, new universes are created, each of which contains a clone of you. Before the split you were one person, and although you are still one person afterwards, you exist in more than one universe. Although each universe has an identical past, shaped by events prior to the split, after the split each operates in its own way. In other words, you exist in this world and react to events as they unfold in it, at the same time as you are also reacting to different events in different worlds. No contact can be made between these universes, but if you exist in each you do not need to make contact anyway.

## Cross-universe travelling

Do you make contact with these other universes in your dreams? When you are sleeping, you are divorced from the external stimuli of this world and should therefore be able to experience the other universes that you inhabit. Since you are the same, you would not experience a feeling of strangeness, but *would* experience a different universe.

Perhaps this theory could also explain prophetic dreams. If you enter a universe that is parallel to your own, but which is a future universe, and observe something that is significant to you personally or on a global scale, you should be able to identify something in your present existence that will happen in your present world's future.

### More Information

If you follow this theory to its logical conclusion, you could be experiencing anything from one to a billion different universes during the course of your dream.

# GLOSSARY

**Amplification** Jung's method of selecting each dream symbol and describing what it means to you by relating it to the archetypes, mythology, religion, history, and your own psychology, and then connecting this interpretation to your present life.

**Apnoea** partial or entire suspension of respiration during sleep.

**Archetype** an innate concept or idea which, irrespective of race, culture, creed, or sex, is universally understood.

**Astral projection** the experience of leaving the physical body and viewing the world from a position divorced from the mental self in an "astral" body with its own consciousness and sensory organs.

**Circadian** referring to vital processes that take place in animals and plants in recurring cycles of approximately 24 hours.

**Collective unconscious** a term used to describe aspects of the psyche that are inherited and common to everyone.

**EEG** abbreviation for electroencephalograph, which is used to measure and record variations in electrical potential in different parts of the brain.

**Ego** the part of the personality that is consciously recognized as "I" or "me".

**Existentialism** a philosophical movement that emphasizes the active use of will, not reason, to confront the problems of a non-moral universe.

**Free association** a means of revealing unconscious processes by encouraging spontaneous association of ideas.

**Gestalt** a German word, meaning "form", used to describe an integrated whole that is more than the sum of its parts.

**Hypnogogia** visions or hallucinations experienced just before falling asleep.

**Hypnopompia** visions experienced just before waking.

**Id** the unconscious pleasure principle that acts independently of logic, reality, and morality, driving you to act as you desire.

**Incubation** the conscious planning and production of a dream.

**Lucid dreaming** being consciously aware that you are dreaming while continuing to dream.

**Mandala** a figure comprising both a circle and a square divided into four segments (or multiples of four) that radiate from the centre. The mandala symbolizes the wholeness of the self.

**Mantra** a syllable, word, or verse that has mystical or spiritual power and that is sounded aloud or internally, once or repeatedly.

**Neurotransmitters** chemicals within the body that transmit nervous impulses throughout the central nervous system.

**Parasomnia** a classification for various disorders experienced during sleep, including sleepwalking, night terrors, nightmares, and bedwetting.

**Persona** the mask that you show to the world, your social self.

**Phyletic memory** the collective memory of a species.

**Prodromal dream** a dream that signals that an impending disease may strike the body.

**Psyche** the term for all mental processes, unconscious as well as conscious.

**Psychosomatic** the inter-relationship of mind and body, with special reference to disease.

**Psychospiritual** the psychological aspects of spirituality.

**REM sleep** rapid-eye-movement sleep, when most dreams occur.

**Repression** the exclusion from the consciousness of any painful or antisocial psychic material, such as discomforting memories, desires, or impulses, which then manifests itself in the unconscious mind, often during dreams.

**Self** a term coined by Jung for the core personality, into which all of the other parts of the psyche are integrated.

**Shadow** Jung's term for the part of the self that remains unconscious because it is repressed by the superego.

**Superego** the restraining inner voice of society, parental influence, and your own conscience.

# Further Reading

A. ADLER, *The Practice and Theory of Individual Psychology*, Harcourt, 1927.

BETTY BETHARDS, *The Dream Book*, Element Books, 1997.

MEDARD BOSS, *The Analysis of Dreams*, Rider, 1957.

ROSALIND CARTWRIGHT, *Night Life*, Prentice Hall, 1977.

GAYLE DELANEY, *All About Dreams*, HarperCollins, 1998.

WILLIAM DEMENT, *Some Must Watch While Some Must Sleep*, W. H. Freeman, 1974.

G. WILLIAM DOMHOFF, *Finding Meaning in Dreams*, Plenum Publishing Group, 1996.

ANN FARADAY, *Dream Power*, Berkeley Books, 1997.

PETER FENWICK & ELIZABETH FENWICK, *The Hidden Door: Understanding and Controlling Dreams*, Berkeley Publishing Group, 1999.

DAVID FONTANA, *The Secret Language of Dreams*, Pavilion Books, 1994.

SIGMUND FREUD, *The Interpretation of Dreams*, Penguin Books, 1976.

CALVIN S. HALL, *The Meaning of Dreams*, McGraw Hill Book Co., 1966

ERNEST HARTMAN, *Sleep and Dreaming*, Little Brown & Co., 1970.

C. G. JUNG, *Memories, Dreams, Reflections*, Routledge & Kegan Paul, 1963.

STEPHEN LABERGE, *Lucid Dreaming*, Jeremy P. Tarcher, 1985.

DAVID F. MELBOURNE & KEITH HEARNE, *Dream Oracle: A Unique Guide to Interpreting Message-Bearing Dreams*, New Holland, 1999.

FREDERICK PERLS, *Gestalt Therapy Verbatim*, Bantam, 1971.

LORI REID, *The Dream Catcher*, Element Books, 1997.

ANTHONY SHAFTON, *Dream Reader*, State University of New York Press, 1995.

JEREMY TAYLOR, *Dream Work*, Paulist Press, 1983.

MONTAGUE ULLMAN & NAN ZIMMERMAN, *Working With Dreams*, Hutchinson, 1983.

ROBERT VAN DE CASTLE, *Our Dreaming Mind*, Aquarian Press, 1994.

# Useful Addresses

**American Academy of Sleep Medicine**
6301 Bandel Road NW, Suite 101
Rochester, MN 55901, USA
Tel: (507) 287 6006
Fax: (507) 287 6008
E-mail: aasm@aasmnet.org
www.aasmnet.org

**The Association for the Study of Dreams**
P. O. Box 1166
Orinda, CA 94563, USA
Tel: (925) 258 1822
Fax: (925) 258 1821
E-mail: asdreams@aol.com
www.asdreams.org

**The British Sleep Foundation**
10 Cabot Square, Canary Wharf
London, EH14 4QB, UK
Tel: (207) 345 3317
E-mail: bsf@uk.ogilvypr.com
www.cix.co.uk/~bsfweb

**Canadian Sleep Society**
3080 Yonge Street
Ste 5055/3080, rue Yonge
Bureau 5055, Toronto
ON, Canada M4N 3N1
Tel: (416) 483 6260
Fax: (416) 483 7081
www.css.to

**The Delaney & Flowers Dream and Consultation Center**
P. O. Box 27173 San Francisco, CA
94127, USA
Tel: (415) 587 3424
E-mail: gayle@gdelaney.com
www.gdelaney.com

**European Association for the Study of Dreams (E.A.S.D.)**
39 rue Henri Maus
B4000 – Liège 1, Belgium
Tel: (32) 42 53 03 57
www.oniros.fr/assoceasd

**European Sleep Research Society**
BKH Universitätsstr. 84
D-93042 Regensburg, Germany
Tel: (49) 941 941 1500
Fax: (49) 941 941 1505
E-mail: juergen.zulley@bkr-regensburg.de
www.esrs.org

**Novato Dream Library & Archive**
P. O. Box 866
Novato, CA 94948, USA
Tel: (415) 898 2559
http://members.aol.com/dreammzzz/ncdarch.htm

# INDEX

# ACKNOWLEDGEMENTS

The author would like to gratefully acknowledge the assistance, support, contributions, and advice of Lucy Colman, Jill Davies, Colin Graham, Virginia Kidd, Julia Lawless, Jackie Loxton, Robbie and Glynn Macdonald, Lori Reid, Carol Rudd, and Dr. Kamath, and all those dream analysts who continue to inspire and educate.

The publisher would like to thank John Butler for reading and commenting on the text.

**The Bridgeman Art Library, London**: 35 The Victoria and Albert Museum, London; 38/9 Botticelli *Venus and Mars*, The National Gallery, London; 42B The Louvre, Paris; 74/5 Riberia Jacob's *Dream*, Prado, Madrid. **AKG, London**: 42, 43 The Louvre, Paris, 44, 46, 47, 50 Paul Gauguin *L'Enfant Endormi*, 52, 59 A. Bocklin, *Island of the Dead*, Leipzig Museum de Bilden Keunste, 89, 146, 194. **© Adelchi Riccardo Mantovani/AKG, London**: 46 *Diptychon*, 1975, 47 *Die Agonie der Quellnymphe*, 1975, 146 *Ikarus*, 1988. **Corbis, London**: 23 Paul A Souders; 26 Pablo Corral V; 27 Bettmann. **Hulton-Getty Images**: 48. **Images Colour Library, London**: 92. **The Image Bank, London**: 76, 81, 197, 202. **The Science Photo Library**: 216. **Stone/GettyOne**: 8, 54T, 54B, 55T, 64 ,82, 198, 203, 206, 214. **The StockMarket, London**: 14, 62, 164.